My Everyday Lagos

My Everyday Lagos

Nigerian Cooking at Home and in the Diaspora

Yewande Komolafe

Photographs by Kelly Marshall
Location Photographs by Lọlá Ákínmádé
Illustrations by Diana Ejaita

TEN SPEED PRESS
California | New York

CON TENTS

Yorùbá Glossary

Here is a choice selection of words in Yorùbá and their closest English translations, all of which you'll find within these pages.

àádùn
a toasted corn snack

agége bread
a pillowy soft white bread

àkàrà
hot bean fritters, usually a celebration food

àlapa
a brothy version of the basic ọbẹ̀ ata sauce

àmàlà
fermented yam powder

àsáró
a porridge made from a starchy root vegetables in a seasoned broth

àṣẹ́
a word of power and affirmation with myriad meanings depending on context

ata dín dín or buka stew
caramelized relish

ata lílọ̀
fresh pepper sauce

bàbá dúdú
coconut milk caramels

beniseed
sesame seed

buka
street food joint

dawadawa powder
a spice made from fermented locust beans

dòdò
fried sweet plantains

dòdò Ìkírè
fried sweet plantains coated in a spice mix

èbà
a swallow made from fermented cassava coarse ground flour

efirin
a type of basil (a.k.a. *scent leaves*)

ẹ̀gúsí seed
melon seed

ẹ̀kọ
fermented corn porridge (a.k.a. *pap*)

ẹ̀kọ tutu
a fermented and steamed corn pudding

ekuru
steamed bean pudding or bean cake made without red palm oil

ẹ̀wà agoyin
cooked, mashed honey beans with a chile sauce

ẹ̀wà àsepọ̀
one-pot meal of beans and starchy vegetables cooked together

ẹ̀wà olóyin
a variety of honey beans that are slightly sweet when cooked

ẹ̀wà rírò
stewed beans

ẹ̀wà sísè
cooked mashed beans

ewúró
bitter leaf

flours
  àmàlà (from dehydrated yam or plantain flours)

  fùfú (from dehydrated cassava flours)

  garri (from fermented cassava coarse ground flour)

  iyán (from pounded yam)

fùfú
(foofoo, foufou)
see *swallow*

gbègìrì
bean soup (a.k.a. *miyan wakye* in Hausa)

gbúre
waterleaf

groundnut
peanut

ilá
okra

ìkókoré
type of àsáró made with water yams

kaun
potash (can be substituted with baking soda)

koko
cooked porridge formed into dumpling-like mounds

Kuti, Fela Anikulapo (1938–1997)
the musician and activist who, with his band Koola Lobitos, was a pioneer of Afrobeat, a fusion of African music and American funk and jazz

móín móín
a pureed bean paste wrapped and steamed in leaves

obè ata
spicy stew

obì
kola nut

ògi
raw paste of fermented corn starch; also sometimes referred to as the porridge made from the paste (èko)

òka baba
a paste made of sorghum

òjòjò
water yam fritter

òkèlè
a soft-cooked starch (a.k.a. *swallow* or *fùfú*)

òle
a variety of water lily leaves

òrógbó
bitter kola

sísè
cooked

swallow
a type of soft-cooked starch made from root vegetables or tubers

tanfiri
a snack made from ground peanuts and roast corn (a.k.a. *dankwa* or *danqua*)

tètè
callaloo or amaranth greens

wàrà
deep-fried cheese curds from cow's milk or soybean milk (a.k.a. *wagashi*)

Yemoja, Olókun, and Oṣun
Yorùbá water deities

Yorùbá
the language spoken by the Yorùbá people, a West African group from Nigeria, Benin, and Togo as well as the African diaspora

Welcome to Lagos

My flight to Lagos arrives at dusk, and I slide out to an airport buzzing with activity, commerce, and community. For me, it's also a confusion of crowds after the stillness of a thirteen-hour flight. Once I am in the car, driving to my parents' house, I can see shadows along the roadside, forms emerging from the headlights' edges and plunging back into the darkness. Lagos is a city by the sea, a city with a distinct coastline, islands both natural and man-made, and a never-ending expansion toward what we call "the mainland." Any benefits of an Atlantic Ocean breeze are swallowed up a few miles into the mainland's humidity. Wherever you are in Lagos, the streets are never silent and never still. A quick glance and all seems calm. But when I look out those car windows into the night, people are filling up the dark like a tide rolling in and receding. They're striding, chatting in groups, gathering by a food stand on the edge of a streetlight's glow. They are carrying the city, still bursting with energy and life, steadily into the middle of the night.

As we come up Adeniyi Jones Road, to the small enclave of houses where my parents live, my mother points out landmarks from my childhood. None are immediately recognizable, but her voice is all the familiarity I need: I'm strangely, and impossibly, home. I breathe in the air and feel every inch of my person expand. We step out of the car and are greeted by the heat, the gorgeous glow of old incandescent bulbs in faded sconces, and the foliage filling every spare inch of our yard. Lemongrass, wild oregano, and scent leaf fill the air as I walk up to the front door.

My parents' home in Ikeja, Lagos, is a green oasis built with concrete and glass. From the dining room I can make out the shape of a banana tree in the corner of the garden. Bright yellow star fruit hang low on another tree. Everything is ripe and ready for picking. I hear chickens clucking, settling in for the night.

Dinner is a light meal of stewed meat in ọbẹ̀ ata, fried sweet plantains, braised greens, and steamed rice. The scent leaf I noted in the garden has been julienned, garnishing the dishes. It is my first time back in my parents' home in twenty years. On the plate before me, all of the complexities of a life lived in exile seem intermingled with the simplicity of home.

I had moved to the United States as a student in August of 1998, following in the footsteps of my brother, who had begun university a year before me. I was the middle child, insulated from much of the outside world by two strong-willed and independent brothers. In America, I could rely on my emigration to be guided by the path my older brother was carving out for himself. I could rely on

him to help me study in, and live within, this new environment.

Less than a year after my arrival in America, my brother passed away. He suffered from sickle cell anemia, a disease I have as well, a condition that created a bond between us that extended beyond the typical bond of siblings. We had always been conscious of our limits, and my parents overly protective of them, but in the United States, the world was new to us. We were still finding our way. The disease took him just shy of his twentieth birthday. His death in Newark in 1999 left me devastated and untethered; at seventeen years old, I was alone in a new country.

My college years in Maryland were marked by this grief. I tried to cope by distancing myself from emotion. At this point, the forward movement of my life was not self-driven. I was fulfilling the responsibilities that had been set out for me: study, obtain a degree, and use the education I received. I was raised by two parents with master's degrees from foreign universities, and in a way, there was an understanding that their children would follow in their footsteps.

I moved through college slowly, unsure of myself every step of the way, but I knew that completing my undergraduate degree satisfied my parents. By the time I received my bachelor's degree, I had become what a lot of young immigrants become: a twenty-one-year-old slowly adapting to a new culture and its emphasis on youthful expressions of independence. I became convinced that I had fulfilled my obligation to my parents. Immediately after

college, I announced I was going to culinary school.

This decision served two purposes: I could embrace something that I had always loved, and I could remain in the United States. The culinary school's structure and student visa gave me the peace of mind to focus my passions. It also gave me valuable tools I still draw on today, an education in the ways food is prepared and presented in the United States, and insights into how food is discussed in the media and in print. What happened in culinary school transformed the next fifteen years of my life, in ways that I could never have imagined.

I came from a four-year college where I did not have to be enrolled in summer courses to keep my status on a student visa. This was not the case in culinary arts school, as I found out during my first summer there. I did not enroll in summer classes and the bursar's office mistook my non-enrollment to mean that I was no longer attending the school. They notified the office of immigration that I was no longer a student at the school. I alerted the school immediately of the mistake, but they were unable to fix it. The machinations of the US immigration system were already in motion: a visa status revoked, a series of letters generated, and a hearing set to order my removal. I would have to leave the country where I had carved out a home for the previous six years.

I didn't.

My life as an undocumented immigrant in the United States is a story that millions of others have lived and experienced. And like all those stories, it has its thread of unique experience. After I decided to stay, I went on to complete my courses at culinary school and began working at restaurants. The restaurant world can be a refuge of sorts for the undocumented. It is also a world that can push grief, suffering, or trauma from the forefront of your consciousness. The intensity of kitchen environments, and the adrenaline rushes they generated, propelled me forward. There was no discussion of my immigration status in the restaurant world. There was no focus on my life as the exile I was slowly becoming.

But I knew too that my sickle cell wouldn't allow me to pull twelve-to-fifteen hour shifts forever. I couldn't live on my feet. Persistent restaurant shifts make demands of the human body and will eventually fully consume it.

My move from restaurants to print publications, test kitchens, and cookbooks was an act of survival, and it is here where parts of my story may diverge from those of other undocumented people in the food industry. I transitioned from an environment populated by others without status, to a world where it quite literally didn't occur to anyone that I would be undocumented.

My workday was different—I began assisting on shoots, styling food, testing recipes for others—but the substance of my work was exactly the same. In restaurants, I cooked the food Americans have come to identify as their cuisine. Although its source material is European, it is modified by indigenous or local ingredients and informed by the contributions of millions of immigrants who've arrived on these shores to inject their culture's food into the assimilation and appropriation that surrounds them. The food I cooked in restaurants was the food I prepped for magazines and cookbooks. It was the food I studied and executed in culinary school. It is the food that people have been highlighting for generations.

My career in food media did not afford me the same distractions as my restaurant work. I began to consciously question whose food I was making. I didn't see myself reflected in it. This is a critical part of work in any field: is our identity part of the substance of our work or are we merely stewards of someone else's? More and more, I began to see that the food I was making for others omitted my own voice. I began to yearn for the food I had made growing up; the food my mother, grandmother, aunties, and ancestors had gifted me.

I married an amazing man in 2016. He—an American with Swiss, Irish, and French-Canadian roots—and I, a Nigerian living in immigration exile in the United States, decided to become a unit. I had spent the past seventeen years moving apartments and states, dragging my knife roll up and down the East Coast. The consistent threat of deportation kept me from placing firm roots down, as I knew I could be removed from the country at any time. Getting married to Mark was the beginning of a process of undoing the damage that living undocumented had done. It meant we could begin the unromantic task of legalizing my status in the United States. More importantly, our relationship provided a space where

I could create roots and build a home. It was a shelter I had not known since losing my older brother.

I created a dinner series in my Brooklyn home that fall. The dinners centered around the food I grew up eating in Lagos, allowing me to revisit so much more than recipes and flavors. I saw the culinary world and its narrow ideas of who gets to tell the story of food. I saw how my food could be just as central as the food I had studied in culinary school. I explored the idea of home while examining the process of adaptation that we undergo as immigrants. I saw my ingredients, the cultivation of those ingredients, their preparation techniques, and their cooking methods as a grave absence within me. I decided to confront that absence.

In 2017, after eighteen years away, I boarded a plane to Nigeria with my husband, filled with nervous anticipation for a place I'd left behind. My process of reconnection is the basis for this book—an embrace of the Nigerian cuisine that I have carried within me. Recoupling with it, learning it from the ground up, and seeking a deeper connection with it has taken me back to the understanding of its fundamental elements. It has been a culinary education suffused by the powers of memory.

This book brings Lagos to the center stage—a city of twenty-plus million inhabitants whose distinct visions of Nigeria, and its food, intermingle and collide. This is the Nigeria I am most familiar with and the city that grew in my imagination. Lagos, like all great cities, is not made of simple adjectives. Its pace is furious. Its course has changed and adapted in my absence, and even in the months between my trips home.

In this book, I'll take you through a full week of Lagos's culinary life—from its harried early morning breakfasts to the midday and nighttime meals at cafes, bukas, street vendors, and home kitchens. Together, we will move through Ikeja, Agége, Mushin, Surulere, Victoria Island, and Lekki, where the culinary identity of a nation intermingles on Lagos's streets. We'll explore ceremonial foods by relaxing into weekend weddings, baby naming celebrations, birthday parties, and other festive occasions. Finally, we'll experience how the year-round warm weather ensures seasons bursting with fresh fruits, vegetables, and herbs, creating opportunities for sweet indulgences and refreshing beverages to satisfy the thirsty souls of the city. A bounty of ingredients creates the flow of life in Lagos, and that flow is fueled by a distinctive and multifaceted cuisine.

I implore you to approach this cookbook not from the perspective of an outsider, as easy as that may be. It is meant to start a conversation, rather than serve as a monologue. Childhood friends of mine who remained in Lagos during the twenty years I spent abroad are informed by something that I was not. This book may be as unique to them as it is to you. To those in the African diaspora, this book highlights food that may have been adapted and integrated into the cuisines of the places they live. The bukas of London, Houston, Atlanta, Chicago, Toronto, and Newark all have their unique vision of Nigeria. This book is not definitive to them, or authentic to

their experience—only mine. But taken in total, this book provides one small contribution to the conversation about what cuisine can be.

I want to underscore that Nigerian food is not confined to the boundaries of our recipes, or the ingredients we use. There are approaches to food shared here that have been left out of the discussions of food in America, and restaurants and food media specifically. They are absent from other cuisines. Nigerian food shares much of the same approaches as other West African cuisines, and what is highlighted here brings those ideas to the forefront. I offer my exploration of Nigerian cuisine in these pages so that you may experience how we eat, why we eat what we eat, and what our food contributes to humanity's palate.

Evolving Lagos

Lagos is a city along the Atlantic Ocean that comprises a coastal mainland and islands, both natural and man-made. Its intricate coastline is shaped by small inlets and expansive lagoons. The exact borders of Lagos are not always clear and are constantly evolving. What might be geographically considered a "coastal city" can feel quite like the opposite after only a few kilometers inland; any benefits of an Atlantic Ocean breeze are swallowed up by the humidity. But there is a continuity between the Lagos islands and the mainland Lagos, and this single identity holds together a city that spreads across hundreds of square miles. Whether that identity is informed by innovation or tradition, overindulgence or deficiency, folly or wisdom, freedom or oppression, the ideals of Nigerian independence or the ghosts of colonialism, the city is embodied in its truest expression by its people. Wherever you are in Lagos, the streets are never silent, never still.

As a child, the seeming endlessness of activity and dynamism make every day a ripe, new adventure. In the morning, the streets are filled by the people who embrace the early part of the day and do what they can to hold onto the tenuous order that is slipping from the city as the day reaches its peak. By noon, the streets have lost that pleasant chaos, having descended into the full-blown disorder of everyday life. The life here ranges from young to old, vibrant to reserved, wildly unpredictable at one corner— where children weave around and slap the cars with hands full of products to sell—to mind-numbingly predictable, as when a long queue of cars snarled in a "go-slow" is your only reality.

Lagos has grown so fast as a city that no neighborhood has remained untouched by its growth, no Lagosian has been able to ignore it. A seemingly endless number of new settlements continue to be carved out of what was once the outskirts of town.

Lagos has distinct class divisions, and those boundaries influence every aspect of life, including its food. Privilege and access may afford one the convenience and luxury of dining out in the city's burgeoning service-based restaurant scene. This access does not define or limit the brilliance of the cuisine itself. The finest Nigerian food available in five-star hotels on Victoria Island may not always taste better than the street side bukas or home kitchens across the mainland. Our cuisine is sophisticated

in its flavor combinations and the quality of its ingredients, not on their prices.

Given that Lagos is an equatorial city, there are two principal seasons: "the wet season" and "the dry season." My favorite is the latter, and especially around the period late in the year and into the New Year when the Harmattan finally reaches Lagos. During the Harmattan, dusty sands from the Sahara settle over everything and hang permanently in the air, obscuring even familiar places from childhood in an aura, into mystery itself. The greenery, so waxen and polished in other seasons, takes on a patina and slightly muted luster. The streetlights are softened by the dusty air, as if you're seeing the night through vintage color television footage.

I have my version of Lagos, and every Lagosian has theirs, but some factors influence us all. I connect to Lagos in my own unique way, shaped by my access to it. I'm fortunate to have grown up there, and to have been afforded the kinds of opportunities that my parents provided for me. I left Lagos as a teenager, and for nearly twenty years could only return to it in memory. I work in food because of the memories my parents gave me of home, not from any assurance that working in kitchens and food media was in any way a viable career. My life in food and my youth in Lagos have many parallels that I continue to draw upon. The role of memory in my cooking is one that I cannot underscore enough. Lagos is the site of those memories, the settings and the moments that primed me for my work. Adulthood in Lagos, as I've come to understand since I've returned, is a balance between the routine and the unfamiliar.

Working in a busy restaurant kitchen is like trying to read a book with an ambulance outside your window: think of a loud, repetitive high-pitched sound that doesn't interrupt the physical work of holding the book, but seems to affect every mental process at once. Though the smells are overwhelming, the lighting bright, and the sounds sharp and sustained, you grow accustomed to them. You adapt to the kitchen. And you develop a responsiveness to extraordinary subtleties—you hear a shallot searing too quickly, its scent building to bitterness. You also develop coping mechanisms for being in that kind of chaos night after night. A chef in a restaurant kitchen, even in the chaos of a dinner rush, knows how to add just the right pinch of salt to something that hasn't been tasted. The kitchen cultivates an extraordinary ability to find focus, attunement, even moments of stillness amidst disarray.

This is how I might describe Lagos to someone who asks me where I am from and what it is like there. Its energy is overwhelming, its chaos and disorder acutely unnerving. But once you adjust to it, you feel as though it heightens your senses. The traffic, even at midnight, can threaten to take the last bit of your day's enthusiasm away from you. But you'll emerge from the car into a late-night hotspot and feel a blossoming energy returned to you. Crises in other places are mere mishaps in Lagos.

Lagos has no more chaos or confusion than other major cities. But Lagos feels to me like a distinctly African megacity, one that preserves its relationship to nature even as it paves over it. Lagos was neither colonized by the Portuguese or English into existence, nor was it born in the decades that followed its independence. For centuries, it has been adapting, expanding, and evolving. For those of us in the diaspora who revisit it in short stays, or only in memory, it is still revealing itself.

Young Nigerians are rediscovering the sentiments that inspired independence and the histories of our people before colonization. In turn, they are reinvigorating every aspect of our society. Bold activists and advocates are courageously using their civic voices and engaging in political struggle, catalyzing urgent questions about who is safe and who is free in Nigerian society. The growing social movements offer reflection for Nigerians across the globe on who we are as a people. As artists, filmmakers, creatives, entrepreneurs, we are all confronting and redefining the relationships we have with ourselves and what we believed our traditions to be. We are constructing a new reality out of the centuries of life that are still preserved within the modernizing cities and towns. We speak a language of conflict and reconciliation, of truth and uncertainty, of daily experience and lifelong tradition. In Lagos, there are places on the map still blank, because neighborhoods appeared faster than the maps could name them. For me, in Lagos, change is a force that simultaneously reimagines the present and the past. In this reality, I am wary of making any kind of definitive statement through my cuisine.

I can still see my grandmother hunched over a pot in the backyard of her home in Surulere, tending the flames to ensure that into the jollof rice would seep a smokiness that no stovetop or sauce in a jar can replicate. I see my mother at Oyíngbo Market in Ebute Metta, hand-selecting the finest herbs and dried plants for making medicines. I see my aunt in her kitchen in Ikeja unwrapping a yaji spice that is quite literally the best on the planet. There is a brilliant and defiant order to Lagos, and it starts with its people, and it stems from their relationships with each other. From that simple context outward, Lagos is a place where anything is possible.

THE FLAVOR ESSENTIALS OF NIGERIAN CUISINE

Smoked Catfish

Crayfish

Panla
(Stockfish)

Coconut Oil

Red Palm Oil

Irú & Ogiri

Shawa

Groundnut Oil

Chiles

Ginger

Tamarind

Sugarcane

Irú & Ogiri

Ewúró (Bitterleaf)

Chiles

Efirin (Scent Leaf)

Lemongrass

Peppersoup Spices

These ingredients are the foundation and building blocks of our cooking. Think of them as the core components and essential flavors of the complex and layered dishes that make up our cuisine. Learning them is orienting in some of the fundamentals of Nigerian food. But for me, adapting these culinary foundations is also essential; substitute as you need to make the recipes accessible to your palate and dietary preferences.

A Note on Ingredients

Sourcing ingredients in Lagos can be an adventure. Finding the best elements for a dish may require a whole team of purveyors and mentors—people who know where to go, when to get there, and who to talk to. As throughout West Africa, finding ingredients relies on a web of social relations and word of mouth among trusted sources. In the diaspora, sourcing ingredients can be like putting together a jigsaw puzzle. This is not meant to dissuade you, but to encourage you to discover the art and relationships of ingredient sourcing in your own immediate context. I've learned that cooking Nigerian food requires enlisting the counsel of those in the know at *some* point, even if you've been doing it your whole life. This likely has to do with our oral traditions and knowledge exchange—cuisine is sacred knowledge passed on orally and through hands-on learning, almost a form of apprenticeship to the long-standing combinations and preparations at the base of our culinary culture.

I am not, and have never been, an expert on Nigerian cuisine. I put my faith in the expertise of others. Wherever Nigerians are, there are likely to be shops, markets, and restaurants that feature our cuisine. The adventure of the search for ingredients was the first means by which I connected with the cuisine of home. It became, and still remains, an obsession.

In 2004, fresh out of college and at the infancy of my culinary education, I took a job at a Nigerian restaurant outside of Baltimore, Maryland. To this day the owner, Olamidé, is a dear friend and an invaluable resource for whenever I want to scale a recipe into multiple batches, source an obscure spice, or when I need a dish to deliver a taste of home in a way only she would know how to execute.

In the summer of 2017, I drove from Williamsburg, Brooklyn, to Moab, Utah, and back. Later that summer I flew to California and spent a month working on cookbooks in Los Angeles and San Francisco. On those two trips, America felt new to me in a way that it hadn't since I'd arrived in Newark, New Jersey, as a sixteen-year-old. For me America had always felt like a collection of the few cities that I had lived in, connected by crowded interstates and the rented U-Hauls that moved me from one culinary outpost to another.

But on my drive out west, I connected the spaces in between. I felt for the first time the joy of hiking through national parks, of driving the two-lane state routes through wide open country, and exploring the eclectic cuisines of so many immigrant communities who'd found a place in America and brought their connections to home with them.

And through them—the supply networks they established, the restaurants they opened, and the lives they built for themselves in business and education—I discovered my own cuisine, and how it had moved, adapted, and thrived wherever it arrived: a market in Charlottesville; restaurants in Charlotte,

Houston, Denver, and Albuquerque; genuine bukas in Atlanta, Chicago, Newark, and Brooklyn.

When I think about what the vast community of Nigerians has done to preserve and recreate our cultures, well, not only am I stunned, but I am moved beyond words. A network of both formal and informal suppliers keeps us connected to our homeland and allows us to create extraordinary food. Inspired by this collective resourcefulness, I returned to New York after my summer of travel and set out to develop a supply network of my own.

African grocery stores are places you should return to again and again. Keep in mind that while colonially imposed borders distinguish our nationalities, many of the ethnicities and cultures alive and vibrant in Nigeria exist in neighboring countries of West Africa. So if you can't find a specifically Nigerian grocery, it's still worth exploring perhaps an Ivorian, Cameroonian, Ghanaian, or "African" grocer to start. Beyond locating the right ingredients, however common or obscure, it's the familiarity that we reconnect with in African grocers that feels like home is never far away. These stores are always lively, with owners, employees, neighbors, and customers coming and going, catching up loudly in their dialects, sometimes with local or international television or radio programs playing. The items for sale aren't curated like Western groceries, so you may have to ask to be guided through a crowded maze or stacks of products to uncover what you're seeking. Regular clients or "cousins" stop in to chat, and you may almost certainly have to interrupt someone in order to seek the assistance you need; there's rarely a sense of timeliness or urgency. African groceries may be demarcated by different nationalities, but one thing that these stores share is a certain communal chaos, a bustling and boundless energy that will certainly remind anyone who identifies as "African" fondly of their version of "home"—a through-line carried by our food and market cultures that evokes a fulfilling familiarity with every visit.

If you're sourcing these ingredients for the first time, the Nigerian restaurateurs in your area will know which stores to go to, and there are online purveyors who specialize in the traditional foods of peoples across Nigeria. Since Nigerians living abroad usually cannot survive without good Nigerian food, they may be the resource I trust the most when initiating the quest to find "the right" ingredients. Start there, with your Nigerian friends, or their parents or aunties. Wherever you go, let the process invite you to connect not just with the products and produce, but the *people*—Nigerian or otherwise—who keep culinary cultures alive in your own neighborhoods, boroughs and cities.

Plant-Based Eating in Nigerian and African Cuisine

While you'd be hard-pressed to find foods across African cultures that are explicitly called "vegetarian" or "vegan," plant-based diets and dishes have had a long history in Nigerian cuisine and on the continent. There are plenty of non-meat options and adaptations in which meat is absent and not missed. Much like what is referred to as "superfoods" in Western markets, "vegetarian" or "vegan" aren't always accurate labels to describe our food.

I've found that in most of Nigerian cuisine, meat is often used as an ingredient for flavor in dishes, not as the focus. Our cornerstone flavors, such as ferments, herbs, and spices, are so crucial to our cuisine, dishes can easily be adapted without meat and are no less satisfying. While new approaches may be questioned, and traditional ways of making beloved recipes championed, vegetables are not just replacing meat in these recipes; they reveal different paths to familiar flavors.

Techniques that build and layer flavor are important, regardless of whether the dish is vegetarian or not. Dishes such as Èwà Sísè (page 58) with beans and onions stewed soft enough that they fall apart, melting into a sauce or alternatives like Wàrà (page 48), or a soup like Miyan Taushe (page 235) with chunks of softened sweet squash in a peanut sauce are all complex and vegetable forward without being labeled as such.

In most cases, plant-based eating aligns with a more traditional way of life, where the cuisine is typically informed by access and a diversity of ingredients. Although certain ingredients such as pork may be avoided, religious observance and vegetarianism are not always strictly linked. Privilege facilitates the notion that one can eat solely vegetarian. Choosing to eat a solely meat-free diet is tied more to privilege than practicality.

THE CORE INGREDIENTS OF NIGERIAN CUISINE

PRESERVED FISH

Preserved fish in Nigerian cuisine takes two primary forms: smoked and dried. Both methods intensify the flavor.

Fish may need to be picked over and cleaned when you get home. Smaller portioned fish, like herring, will have bones that do not need to be removed. Larger species of dried fish, like North Atlantic cod, will require some deboning.

If you're not familiar with preserved fish, allow yourself some grace and fun in experimenting with what you can find around you. In addition to African grocers, Caribbean markets and local fish markets are great places to start.

DRIED CRAYFISH

In Nigerian cuisine, crayfish is a cornerstone ingredient. Crayfish can vary in size and can be found milled into a coarse powder or whole. For these recipes, I've used tiny whole crayfish and most of the recipes that call for crayfish here are referring to the smallest ones that you can find. When using crayfish powder in place of whole crayfish, simply halve the amount called for because ground crayfish releases stronger flavors. Crayfish can be substituted with tiny dried shrimp.

RED PALM OIL

I always keep red palm oil in my pantry. It is a central ingredient for making the food that transports me home. Though mildly floral at first taste, it blossoms slowly as it coats your tongue, revealing an almost smoky presence. Its bright orange smear coating an empty bowl is like nothing I can achieve with other ingredients. Visually, texturally, and of course by way of flavor, it has a power which I ascribe to few other pantry items.

Red palm oil has always had culinary and medicinal uses. Its unrefined form is packed with beta carotenes. A rich source of vitamin A, E, and K, it has a long history as a means of addressing fevers and inflammation. In most West African countries, it is produced and used locally. Nigerian agriculture is primarily small scale in a way that is hard for most Westerners to comprehend. Nigeria lacks both large processing capabilities and the necessary transportation infrastructure to harvest and refine palm oil at the scale necessary to compete with other palm oil-producing nations. Because oil palm trees are part of the native forests of West Africa, their cultivation does not involve deforestation, habitat destruction, or any of the hallmarks of industrial-scale farming.

MANSHANU

Manshanu is an ingredient mostly used in northern Nigerian cuisine that adds creaminess and gloss to a variety of dishes. It is ideal for sautéing ingredients or finishing sauces. Slightly fermented, it carries a lovely, mild funk. Manshanu will keep well when stored refrigerated in an airtight container for up to a month. You can make your own following my recipe on page 96 but ghee or animal tallow are easy substitutes.

CANNED TOMATO PASTE

Arriving to Nigeria during the era of colonization, tomato paste hasn't supplanted native ingredients so much as enhanced them. Adding tomato paste to sauces and soups helps bring out the flavors of a variety of other ingredients—from dried fish and meat to bell peppers and Scotch bonnets.

De Rica was such a common brand of tomato paste during the 1970s and 1980s that most recipes would list volume measures for ingredients (including tomato paste) in the number of empty De Rica cans required, as opposed to cups or ounces. The familiar empty cans are still used as a unit of measure in the markets to scoop and measure bulk grains, beans, spices, and other dry ingredients.

HONEY

I have a huge 3-liter jar of Nigerian honey in my pantry. What I refer to as "Nigerian honey" is not a universally applicable term, as every honey's flavor depends upon the nearby flora. The honey I source in Lagos is always deep and dark in color. In the United States, buckwheat honey is a close substitute.

Honey rounds out flavors in our cuisine. I use it often to finish dishes because the flavor is robust, bold, and complex, with malt-like notes and a molasses-like finish. It's not as sweet as blonder honeys, and tends to add savoriness to dishes.

BELL PEPPERS

Red bell peppers are the most popular, or perhaps more broadly used pepper in our sauces and stews. A number of red bell peppers—tatashe (fresh paprika) being one of them—are indigenous and local to Nigeria. You can experiment with local varieties available to you. When recipes call for bell pepper, I am usually referring to the variety of red bell peppers found in most grocery stores and markets in the United States. Green bell peppers are also used in Nigerian soups and stews, and are usually milled or chopped as garnishes.

TAMARIND

Tamarind is fruity, earthy and adds a layer of mild acidity to dishes. Tamarind is available as whole pods, pulp, or store-bought purees or syrups. To make your own puree, soak the pods in hot water and press the pulp through a sieve (see page 98). Discard the pods and seeds and store the concentrate in the refrigerator. Stir into soups and stews to brighten and finish dishes.

Pre-made tamarind purees and syrups are easily found in African, Asian, or Latin groceries. If you are purchasing these, be careful. There are a variety of products with different concentrations—some incredibly strong and tangy, and others fruity and mild—so you may need to try a few to find the ones best suited for accenting dishes and experiment with the right proportions.

FRESH AND DRIED CHILES AND PEPPERS

Fresh, smoked, and dried chiles are abundant throughout Nigeria and across West Africa. The most common fresh chiles are Scotch bonnets, where every color (red, green, yellow, or orange) is used. Dried chiles can pack a punch with only a few seeds, and each carries a different oil and fragrance. Some examples of dried chiles or peppers used include Selim peppercorns, alligator peppers, smoked Cameroonian peppers (yellow Scotch bonnets), cayenne (green and red), uziza seeds, and grains of paradise. While some of these are very unique to West Africa, you can experiment with New Mexican and other Southwestern dried chiles, fresh habaneros, serranos, jalapeños, and others that are readily available in your area.

LEAFY GREENS AND HERBS

Nigeria's land is rich and fertile, with an abundance of herbs and greens. In the North, the seasons are shorter, so greens are often dried and preserved for year-round use. Similar dried greens can be found in African groceries and markets in the diaspora. A lot of the greens used in these recipes will be available this way. Just be sure to clean and rehydrate these before use. Our indigenous greens can also be substituted with mature spinach, collards, turnip, dandelion, or mustard greens—really any greens that can stand up to cooking and stewing. Oko Farms in Brooklyn, New York, has been an extraordinary resource for me, allowing me to source and cook with fresh heirloom greens and herbs—and benefit from their medicinal qualities—throughout the year. However, for those without access to an extraordinarily gifted farmer friend, rest assured that substitutions will work. If you have access to a local farmer's market or CSA, "mixed braising greens" are always a solid option for these recipes.

Ẹ̀GÚSÍ SEED, ESA (BENNE) SEED, AND GROUNDNUT THICKENERS

Ẹ̀gúsí seeds are the seeds of a melon indigenous to West Africa. The protein-rich seeds act as an ingredient on their own, but they also help with the consistencies of our sauces and stews. Ẹ̀gúsí and esa (benne seeds) can be used whole or ground into a powder or paste in soups like Ẹ̀gúsí Soup (page 172). Groundnuts or peanuts can be found coarse-ground raw or roasted, and like esa, are thickeners that add flavor and heft to dishes like Miyan Taushe (page 235) and Kunu Gyada (page 243). You can grind your own unsalted, raw, or roasted peanuts at home.

IRÚ, OKPEI, AND OGIRI

Our famous fermented locust beans, known as irú in Yorùbá, are a regional staple that can be smelled and experienced long before they arrive on your plate. They transmit a distinctive umami to any dish, and a little bit goes very far. You may find irú, okpei, or ogiri referred to interchangeably—the difference is in the base seeds and the level of processing they undergo before fermentation. These fermented seeds are essential to these recipes. Make sure the ferments you purchase are pungent and malty, but not sour or saline. Smelling freshly fermented locust beans should be an experience in and of itself—it is intense. Irú may be sold as dawadawa, and is commonly found in northern Nigeria in both dried and powdered forms.

Okpei is a castor oil seed, fermented in a similar manner to irú. Traditionally used in dishes from the Southeast, it adds robust flavors to soups and stews.

Ogiri is fermented benne seed, which is an heirloom sesame. The seeds are sometimes ground before fermentation, resulting in a dark, dried, dense paste sold in large or small chunks. Ogiri is much oilier and more pungent than its locust bean cousin, irú.

COCONUT

Coconuts are plentiful throughout Nigeria, especially across the coastal south. The milk, water, and flesh— either fresh or dried and milled into flour—are widely used in savory and sweet dishes.

SMOKED CAMEROONIAN CHILE PEPPERS

Cameroonian chile peppers are highly seasonal, and can be sourced fresh at the markets in Lagos throughout the year. But you can find them smoked and dried year-round. They add an ethereal smokiness and a caramelly bite to any dish. I rely on one of my aunties for these, as she has a near sixth-sense for when the seedpods will appear in the markets.

EHURU, OR CALABASH NUTMEG

Calabash nutmeg should have a slightly sweet, woodsy aroma, and its flavor profile is distinct from common nutmeg used elsewhere. It is a staple spice in Toasted Peppersoup Spice (page 99) and is used in condiments and spiced butters. It is especially wonderful with delicately flavored ingredients like seafood and poultry.

AIDAN FRUIT

Dried aidan fruit is a warming spice; its fragrance is sweet, and its flavor profile is earthy and round. It is easiest to find in whole pods, which you can steep in broth. Aidan fruit has a long history of medicinal use for a variety of conditions, and is wonderful as an extract for teas and tinctures.

OGBONO SEEDS

Ogbono seeds are very high in fat and will go rancid quickly if not stored properly. Check the seeds for freshness before using. A soapy smell or taste means the seeds are rancid and should not be used. To store, keep whole or ground seeds in an airtight container for up to a month in the freezer.

UDA SEEDS

Uda seeds, or grains of selim, are a musky type of pepper that adds an essential depth and warmth to a variety of soups and stews. The seeds or seed pods are usually smoked.

KAUN (POTASH)

Used in small quantities as a tenderizer for meats or thickener in soups and stews, potash is a food additive that lends a unique texture and mouthfeel. It's fairly neutral in flavor. Baking soda diluted in a small amount of water could act as a sufficient substitute. See page 209.

A PRIMER ON STARCHES

As the companion dishes to our many boldly flavored soups, stews, and condiments, starches are commonly served unadorned, acting as neutral vessels, offering nutritional variety and a range of textures to meals. Methods of preparation and cooking starches can span from the simple (boiling or steaming) to the more complex (pounding or fermenting). All are explored in this section, and this chapter lays the foundation for how our dishes are presented, experienced, and paired.

PLANTAIN

Plantains are as famous as yams in West African cuisine. These starchy vegetables cook fast and can withstand a variety of preparations depending on their stage of ripeness, making them very versatile. Plantains sweeten as they ripen, which affects their starchiness, elasticity, and texture. Green plantains are firm in texture and range in taste from unsweet to mildly sweet. They are typically boiled, grated, or fried for chips. Ripe plantains have skins ranging from yellow with black spots to completely blackened. As they ripen, plantains also soften. Sweet plantains pair beautifully with the spices and acids in many of our stews and are arguably best for frying, though pounded sweet plantains add a lovely mild sweetness to any meal. When purchasing to cook the same day, select plantains with an even yellow or yellow with black speckles and spots on the skin, or even darker if you're looking for a sweet treat.

YAM

Whenever I mention "yams" in this book, I'm referring to an absolute staple in our cuisine: the West African yam. Hailing from what's known as the "Yam Belt," which cuts through the West African subregion (including Benin, Cameroon, Côte d'Ivoire, Ghana, Nigeria, and Togo), these starchy yams are large, oblong, and quite heavy. The average yam weighs two to three pounds and has a rough, thick, slightly hairy brown exterior which must be carefully removed with a knife or peeler to reveal its bright white, pale, or yellow flesh. These starchy yams offer a delightful range of textures: they're soft and tender when boiled, smooth and creamy when crushed into a stew, fluffy and airy when pounded. They are also milled into yam flour which is used for swallow (see page 52 for a guide to swallows). Yams carry a subtle sweetness that complements the pungent and pronounced flavors of our stews, sauces, and condiments. They're equally delightful eaten plain, or boiled in salted water and pounded into a sticky fúfú for stew.

When selecting yams, check for freshness by inspecting the skin for soft spots or indentations, which indicate rot. You want yams that are evenly firm along the surface. It's okay if their exteriors are a bit sandy, as these tubers grow underground and are not sold waxed. You can also find similar yam substitutes in Asian, Caribbean, or Hispanic markets: look for yellow yams, which will be nearly identical in appearance. Yams keep well in cool, dim, dry areas for up to three months.

As you clean and prepare yams, keep a large bowl of water nearby to prevent them from browning. After peeling and chopping each piece, simply submerge them in the water. Yams can be stored in water for up to twelve hours in the refrigerator for advance preparation.

CASSAVA

Cassava is a unique and delightful starch, among the most widely consumed in Nigeria. Their leaves are also edible and used for vegetable soups. These tubers have tough, coarse, waxy brown exteriors which must be removed with a peeler or peeling knife before cooking. Once peeled, their bright flesh is slightly sticky and slippery. The texture changes based on the preparation, and they have a distinctly savory flavor.

Cassava is hardy and can be slightly stringier in texture than some of these other starches. As with yam, you want to select fresh cassava roots that are firm to touch without soft spots, indentation, or visible blemishes. You will find cassava commonly referred to in other African countries as manioc, and as yucca in Latin America. Cassava is the base of tapioca pearls, which are commonly cooked into a porridge in Nigeria. It is also ground, fermented, dried and crushed into garri, a dried powder or coarse flour which accompanies many dishes. A Brazilian version of garri called farinha is further

roasted and served slightly finer in texture than garri. Cassava must also be peeled and cut to remove its narrow core before cooking. Take into consideration that the skin is very thick and coarse—so while not just any vegetable peeler may do the trick, a knife should work just fine. After peeling, cut the root in half lengthwise, then cut the halved pieces in half lengthwise. This way you can easily trim the inner-edge of each wedge to remove the core. The core can also be removed once cooked or left in altogether.

COCOYAM (TARO ROOT)

Cocoyam, or taro root, is another brown tuber, small and bulbous in shape. They must be peeled with a knife or strong vegetable peeler before cooking. Alternatively, you can boil them with the skin on then remove the skins once cooled. They are soft and mild in flavor, with a delicate texture, and they do particularly well in stews where they cook down.

SWEET POTATOES

Like plantains, sweet potatoes offer a lovely sweetness that helps balance the umami and spice in our many condiments, and pairs nicely with seafood. There are dozens if not more varieties worldwide—the kind most commonly found in Nigeria are yellow on the inside, with pale, or light brown exteriors. Japanese sweet yams are the closest variety I have found in the United States, but really any sweet potato will do for boiling or roasting. Sweet potatoes can be boiled with the skins on, or peeled in advance.

Select firm sweet potatoes with no soft spots, and check for rot on the surface of the skin and in crevices.

CORN

Corn is a staple ingredient in Nigerian cuisine, and there are several varieties that are accessible at markets across Lagos. Wherever you see corn in this cookbook, it is safe to assume we are not referring to American sweet corn, which has a much higher sugar content than the maize used in West African cuisine. This is important because of the textures that you're seeking with some of these preparation styles. The corns we use are similar to the masa used to make tortillas. Moreover, they're starchier and tougher than sweet corn, often first dried then ground into various flours, or cooked fresh with a lingering coarseness.

You'll find corn in every stage of processing, including on the cob and fire-roasted; coarse and unprocessed kernels; and fine white glutinous corn flour that can be stirred or steamed, then molded into dense mounds to serve alongside stews and condiments. Cornmeals and flours are cooked into porridges (sometimes fermented first), formed into thick swallows to soak up spicy sauces, or prepared into doughs and fried for snacking.

Canned hominy or specific dried heirloom varieties can be used. Wherever possible, milled corn flour is ideal, or simply opt for the highest quality cornmeal or corn flour you may find.

GRAINS, LEGUMES, AND PULSES

Our starches also come in the form of grains, many ancient and indigenous, others more recently adopted. Sorghum, millet, and fonio are examples of ancient grains that persist in our diets. Millet and fonio can be easily steamed plain; sorghum and millet are commonly milled into flours, sometimes after roasting them first. These flours are the bases of porridge or swallows, and are sometimes fermented. Then of course, there's rice. More recently adopted into the Nigerian diet, white rice is most commonly prepared as Jollof Rice (page 215). While it isn't currently à la mode to use brown or wild rice for jollof, it's certainly an option.

By way of pulses, our most common beans are cowpeas and honey beans, which tend toward the family of black-eyed peas. Beans are an important source of protein and nutrients, especially when paired with grains. Our beans are often cooked down in stews, milled into dried flours, or crushed into pastes that can then be boiled or steamed. Beans are an ancient food as well, and while perhaps less celebrated, they are very authenti-cally a part of our regional cuisine.

FERMENTS OR PRESSED

Nigerian cuisine integrates fermenta-tion as a preparation step, especially for grains such as corn, millet, and rice, and tubers such as yams and cassava. I like to think of fermentation as a dance with my environment, at times loose and improvisational, but always mea-sured and contained. It is a process in which I can rely on nature to alter an ingredient at its own pace.

In grains specifically, fermentation increases nutrient absorption: our bod-ies have an easier time breaking down foods and unlocking their value once they are fermented. Fermentation also transforms the flavor of foods, from any range of subtle to puckery sour and intensely fragrant.

The recipes that follow offer ways to prepare fermented ingredients for recipes such as Èkọ Tutu (page 66), Ògi (page 42), Sinasir (page 204) and Fura (page 45) that you'll encounter later in the book. Summertime with its warm, humid air is when fermentation is at its quickest. But, if it's not warm where you are, there's still plenty to capture. Fermentation is for any season!

This fermented paste is a base for a toasted northern Nigerian rice cake perfect for sopping up soups and stews. The process is near and dear to my heart, one that has become a routine with my older daughter at home. As a one-year-old, she loved running her fingers through the rice when it was just added to the water. Now, she wolfs down the small puffy rice skillet cakes I make with this paste.

It's important to go with a short grain rice here. The glutinous texture creates a rich framework for absorption in the finished cake. This recipe is a base starter for sides such as Masa (page 136) and Sinasir (page 204)—accompaniments that are perfect for young teething children and adults alike.

After grinding the rice into a paste, leave the mixture to ferment at room temperature. This fermented rice paste will last for up to a month refrigerated. Keep it out of the refrigerator for up to an hour before use.

Fermented Rice Paste

YIELD: 2 CUPS

2 cups short-grain white rice

Place rice in a bowl and cover with 2 inches of water. Cover the bowl with a dish towel and soak for 1 to 4 hours. The rice grains should plump up and break easily after soaking. Using a mesh strainer, completely drain out the soaking liquid and move the grains to a blender. Add in 1½ cups water and puree the soaked rice on high speed to a smooth batter. Move the batter to a clean bowl, cover with a dishtowel, and allow to ferment at room temperature for 24 hours. If you want it rather sour, allow to ferment for up to 24 hours at room temperature, then cover and transfer to the refrigerator to ferment slowly for up to 1 week.

In Yorùbá, ògi refers to a raw paste of fermented cornstarch. In Lagos and across the diaspora, the word ògi may also refer to the cooked porridge that is made using this paste. It's a brilliant example of how the ingredients we use sometimes replace the original name of our dishes (like oatmeal, which in Lagos may be referred to as "Quaker Oats"). This paste can be made with several varieties of corn, but the best corn for ògi is any variety that has a high starch content. Yellow and white corn are most frequently used, but I've made successful batches with New Mexican blue corn and several blush pink varieties I've found through an heirloom corn seller. The blush pink corn makes for a bowl of millennial pink porridge, while the blue corn comes out a near-perfect shade of lilac. Red sorghum grains (also called guinea corn) can be mixed with corn prior to soaking. This increases the nutritional value of ògi, adding essential vitamins like iron and niacin. This variation with red sorghum is called ọka baba.

Ògi
(Fermented
Cornstarch)

YIELD: 1 PINT

2 cups dried whole corn kernels or 3 cups coarsely ground cornmeal, any color

Place the corn in a large bowl and cover completely with 3 inches cold water. Soak for 8 to 12 hours until the corn is plump and slightly soft. Pour off the liquid. If using coarse cornmeal, soak by covering completely with 3 inches of water and allow to sit for 4 hours.

Line a fine-mesh sieve with a muslin cloth. In a blender, working in batches, grind the corn or cornmeal on high to a smooth puree using up to 4 cups room temperature water. Fill a large bowl with about 6 cups fresh water. Place the muslin-lined sieve in the large bowl of water and pour in the corn puree. Allow the bottom of the sieve to sit in the bowl of water and stir the puree with your fingers or a wooden spoon. The starch will pass through leaving the chaff in the muslin cloth. The water in the bowl should be cloudy and look milky. Transfer the corn milk to a large stock-pot. Repeat the rinsing and sieving process with fresh water until the milk passing through is almost clear (about 5 rinses). Transfer the milky liquid to the pot after each rinse. Discard the corn chaff after the fifth rinse. Cover the corn milk in the stockpot with a clean kitchen towel and ferment at room temperature. Once fermented, you should notice a slightly sour and sweet smell and bubbles on the surface of the liquid, about 2 to 3 days. Pour off the clear liquid. Stir and transfer the fermented cornstarch to an airtight container, and keep refrigerated. The fermented starch will settle at the bottom of your container and you can discard the clear water. To use, scoop an amount of fermented cornstarch and dissolve in the amount of liquid the recipe calls for.

Fura is a wonderfully simple fermented paste from ground millet. This recipe is the base of the popular northern Nigerian beverage called "fura de nunu" which translates as "fura in milk." The fermented paste can be made with millet or millet flour, and as with most ferments, will develop more flavor by fermenting slowly over time.

Fura
(Fermented Millet Paste)

YIELD: 1 CUP

1½ cups dried millet or 1 cup millet flour

Soak the millet by placing in a bowl and covering the grains up to 2 inches over the top with water. Allow to sit for 1 to 4 hours. Pour off the soaking liquid. In a blender, process the soaked millet with 1 cup room temperature water, on high speed to a smooth puree. (If using millet flour, whisk the flour with 1 cup water in a medium bowl. Cover the bowl with a clean towel and follow the steps to ferment.)

Pour the puree into a medium bowl and cover with a kitchen towel. Allow to sit out on the counter to ferment for 1 to 2 days. If you want it rather sour, ferment for 24 hours at room temperature, transfer to the refrigerator, and allow to slowly ferment for up to 1 week.

Gyada paste is made from soaked raw peanuts—groundnuts in West Africa—which are earthy, creamy, and nutrient-rich. The paste is useful as a thickener in soups, such as Miyan Taushe (page 235), or porridges, such as Kunu Gyada (page 243). It can be stored refrigerated for up to a week, or frozen for up to a month.

Gyada Paste
(Groundnut)

YIELD: 2 CUPS

4 cups fresh, raw peanuts with skin on

Soak the peanuts to rehydrate by placing in a bowl and covering with water up to 2 inches over the top. Allow to sit for at least 1 hour and up to 4 hours until the raw peanuts double in size.

Drain off the soaking liquid using a sieve or colander. In the bowl of a food processor, pulse the rehydrated peanuts and then puree to a smooth paste. You can also do this step using a crushing method in a mortar and pestle. Move the peanut paste to an airtight container with a lid and store in the refrigerator. Gyada paste will keep for up to a week in the refrigerator and for 1 month in the freezer.

Wàrà, also known as wagashi, is a cheese that is filling and creamy, and easily molded and fried as a snack. Most people in Lagos won't bother making wàrà at home since it's widely available marketside, sold fresh or fried as a quick snack lightly dusted with yaji spice. It can also be made at home with a little time and patience. A similar curdled milk version made with soymilk is called "awara" or "beske."

Wàrà can be found across West Africa, and reflects the influence of the Fulani on the cuisines of northern Nigeria, Ghana, Togo, Burkina Faso, and the Nigerian southwest. It can be served as a meat replacement when added to soups and stews. Tofu or paneer can also be used as an adequate substitute for wàrà.

Wàrà (Cow's Milk or Soy Milk Cheese)

YIELD: 8 PIECES

8 cups whole cow's milk or soy milk

¼ cup lemon juice (or 1 tablespoon coagulant enzyme)

Fine sea salt to taste

Pour the milk into a medium saucepan and place over medium-low heat. Warm until the steam begins to rise from the surface, about 4 minutes. Allow to simmer, stirring frequently until the milk begins to thicken and the temperature reaches about 200°F.

While the milk heats, line a fine-mesh sieve with a large square of cheesecloth and set aside. Reduce the heat to low and add the lemon juice. The milk should start to curdle. Remove from the heat and allow to sit without stirring until all the milk has been curdled by the acid, about 10 minutes. Pour into the cheesecloth-lined sieve over a bowl. Strain out the liquid whey by pressing down gently on the solids to remove as much moisture as possible and compress the curd into a cake. You can set a heavy jar right on top of the cheesecloth to help with this process. Allow the cheese to strain and set overnight in the refrigerator.

Once set, peel back the cheesecloth and cut the cheese into eight equal pieces. Pat the pieces dry and season lightly with salt. Store refrigerated for up to 3 days, or immediately follow directions on page 138 to fry.

Garri is a coarsely grated and fermented cassava that has been dehydrated to form flakes or granules. It is dried, then very lightly pan toasted. Garri is commonly sprinkled onto stews throughout Benin, Ghana, Nigeria, and Togo. It is also consumed as a snack when simply soaked in ice water with roasted peanuts (as in this recipe); as a cereal when combined with milk and sugar; as a grain for a light lunch in Burabisco (page 196); or as èbà (òkèlè or swallow) when it is cooked with hot water.

Soaked Garri
(Cassava, Grated and Fermented)

YIELD:
1 SERVING

½ cup Ijebu or ondo garri (see page 51)

1 to 2 teaspoons sugar (optional)

1 tablespoon dry roasted peanuts

Ice cubes, for serving

In a bowl, combine the garri and the sugar if using. Add in 1½ to 2 cups cold water. Top with the roasted peanuts, a few cubes of ice, and serve cold.

Serve alongside any bean dishes or with Whole Roast Fish (page 165), or alone as a refreshing snack.

SOURCING GARRI
(What to Buy)

There are different versions of garri you may come across when sourcing.

Yellow garri is toasted with palm oil to enhance the taste, resulting in a pale yellow granule. This version of garri can be found across Lagos and in the diaspora but originates from the southeastern parts of Nigeria, where palm oil production is also common. Yellow garri is used primarily for making swallow (page 52).

Ijebu garri is made from grated cassava that is fermented slowly to develop a notable and sour, almost acidic taste.

Ondo garri is made from a starchier cassava root, likely driven by the variety of cassava that is grown in the region.

Brazilian Farofa is a variation of finely grated, fermented, and pan toasted cassava granules. It is used primarily as a topping to add crunch to dishes such as Frejon (page 199). It's roots in Brazilian cuisine can be linked to the Africans enslaved there during the Atlantic slave trade.

SWALLOWS
(Òkèlè or Fùfú)

In the same way a spoon carries distinct flavors from the edge of a bowl into its center, or a crust of bread absorbs the essence of the broth in its path, swallows are a means of pulling the best of a dish into each bite.

There is an art to eating swallows—the proper thumb-and-finger pinch to pull off a bite, the almost imperceptible roll of the dough from the palm to the tips of the fingers as it's lowered into soup to scoop a mouthful.

I am highly self-conscious about my swallow-rolling technique, one I've barely improved since my childhood in Lagos. While savoring them effortlessly requires years of practice, shoddy technique does not lessen my appreciation for swallows' subtle, earthy sweetness.

Swallows, as they're called in English, are a broad category of cooked starchy vegetables and grains that are pounded or kneaded until soft and elastic. In regional African and Afro-Caribbean cuisines, they go by a variety of names and are prepared using a range of ingredients; there's northern Nigerian tuwo shinkafa made with rice, East African ugali made from corn, southwest Haitian tonmtonm made from breadfruit.

But perhaps the term most often heard in America is fùfú. All swallows are not fùfú, and fùfú itself ranges in preparation. In Nigeria, fùfú is made from crushed and fermented cassava, sold at markets as a paste to loosen in hot water. Ghanaians may refer to a combination of pounded cassava and additional starches, such as green plantains, as fùfú. In the diaspora, fùfú is most commonly made not by pounding, but by cooking finely milled flours of starchy roots or tubers in hot water on the stovetop. Like most staples, adaptations exist for convenience.

What all swallows share is that they should be served hot, portioned right into a bowl primed for vegetable soups with stewed meats or plastic-wrapped and kept warm for when the meal begins. An accompanying washbowl for rinsing off fingers before and after the meal should always be within reach.

Despite the subtle differences with swallows in West Africa and beyond, eating them leads the way to the very heart of a culinary experience. Swallows alone are not the means to understanding how Lagosians eat, but they begin a conversation—a way to peel back the layers like an endless onion.

Pounding a cooked starch is usually done in a large mortar with a pestle as long as four-to-six feet. Pounding starches is a classic technique learned and perfected over time, and for most Lagosians making swallows this way is sometimes reserved only for special occasions. The process begins with crushing the freshly cooked starch with the pestle, slowly adding hot water to soften the starch. The pestle not only pounds, but also kneads the starch, and the resulting dough has a smooth, glutinous texture like bread dough. Pounded yam is a common starch prepared in this way but plantains, cassava, and rice also get this treatment.

The mortar itself is a work of art, usually carved by hollowing out a cut section of a tree trunk. The pestle is also shaped from a section of a tree trunk. A mortar and pestle of this type, when kept and stored properly, can last several generations.

Pounded Method

SERVES 2

1 pound yam, cassava, sweet potato or green plantains

NOTE In some cases more than one starchy vegetable can be combined to make a blended swallow. Onunu is a swallow made from a combination of pounded yam and ripe plantains. This swallow is from the southern part of Nigeria, a riverine, and is commonly served with a fresh fish stew.

Remove the skin on the yam, cassava or sweet potato by peeling with a paring knife or a vegetable peeler. Cut into 1½-inch pieces and move the peeled roots to a bowl of water to keep from turning brown. In a medium-sized pot, add your peeled starches and cover with water by 2 inches. Bring the pot up to a simmer over medium heat and cook until completely tender, 12 to 15 minutes. Reserve 2 cups of the cooking liquid, then drain out the remaining liquid.

Move the cooked starch to a large mortar and pestle. Pound till crushed to a coarse paste. Add 1 cup of the reserved cooking liquid and continue pounding, adding up to an additional 1 cup reserved cooking water in small quantities at

a time to soften until the paste is a smooth slightly glossy and elastic consistency.

To serve, fill a small bowl with some room temperature water and wet a large serving spoon by dipping it into the water. Divide and shape the dough using the wet spoon to shape into large (3- to 4-inch), slightly rounded balls. Transfer each ball into a shallow bowl as you shape it. Serve alongside Èfó Rírò (page 239) or any of the soups on pages 158–185.

Here, the general technique is to fold the milled flour into water, cooking and stirring with a wooden spoon until a smooth paste is formed. All swallows are not fùfú, but fùfú is the term commonly used in the diaspora to describe the dish in this recipe: continuous cooking, stirring, and kneading turns finely milled starch into a smooth, elastic mass. The resulting swallow, like that of the classic method, is notably neutral in taste and always served warm.

Cooked Flour Method

SERVES 2

1 cup starch flour (see options that follow)

FLOUR OPTIONS
Àmàlà (from dehydrated yam or plantain flours)

Garri (from fermented cassava coarse ground flour)

White yam flour (usually labelled as pounded yam flour)

Semolina (from durum wheat)

Cocoyam flour (from taro root)

Pour 2½ cups of water into a medium sized pot and make a slurry by stirring in the flour all at once. Transfer the pot to the stovetop and set over medium-low heat. Cook the batter stirring as it thickens and begins to form a dough.

Reduce the heat to low and fold the batter over itself with a wooden spoon to mix and smooth out any lumps as you fold. You should have a thick and chalky looking dough at this point.

Cook while mixing until the dough begins to stiffen, pull away from the sides of the pot and a thin film forms on the bottom of the pan, about 3 to 4 minutes. Spread across the bottom of the pot. Use the wooden spoon to poke indents on the surface. Pour in ½ cup water around the edges and over the top of the dough.

Cover and cook, without stirring, over low heat until the dough is heated through, translucent, and all the starchy granules have absorbed the water, about 6 minutes.

Remove the lid and use the wooden spoon to mix into a smooth, slightly glossy and sticky dough. Remove from heat, cover, and allow to sit for 5 minutes to set slightly.

To serve, fill a small bowl with some room temperature water and wet a large serving spoon by dipping it into the water. Divide and shape the dough using the wet spoon to shape into large (3- to 4-inch), slightly rounded balls. Transfer each ball to a shallow bowl as you shape it. Serve alongside any of the soups on pages 158–185.

NOTE The swallows are prepared with no seasoning, not even salt, and as such they are neutral in taste.

POUNDED GRAIN METHOD

Short grain glutinous rice is cooked and pounded in a similar manner to other starches to make tuwo shinkafa, a popular northern "swallow" starch made to accompany soups such as Miyan Taushe (page 235) or Miyan Yakuwa (page 182).

TUWO (Cooked Pounded Rice)

SERVES 2

2 cups short-grain white rice, rinsed and drained

In a small pot, combine the rice and 4½ cups water. Bring to a simmer over medium heat. Lower the heat and cook until the grains are completely tender, about 18–20 minutes.

Using a wooden spoon, mash the rice grains by crushing and folding against the side of the pot. Fold the batter over itself with a wooden spoon to mix and smooth out any lumps as you fold, adding up to ¼ cup of additional water in very small amounts as needed. Continue to fold until the paste is a smooth, slightly glossy, and elastic consistency.

To serve, fill a small bowl with some room temperature water and wet a large serving spoon by dipping it into the water. Divide the dough using the wet spoon to shape into 2 large, slightly rounded balls. Transfer each ball to a shallow bowl as you shape it. Serve alongside any of the soups on pages 158–185.

If not serving immediately, portion into 4-6 spheres and wrap tightly into individual pieces of plastic wrap. Place in a large bowl with a kitchen towel over the portions to keep warm.

BOILED OR STEAMED

Sísè is the Yorùbá word for "cooked in water" and refers to starches that have been boiled or steamed and lightly salted. Sísè is really the simplest way to prepare a starch and cassava, yams, and grains (such as rice, beans, corn, and millet) are examples of popular starches in our diet. As with most cuisines, availability frequently drives use, so picking an accompanying starch for your soup and stew will mostly depend on what's fresh and in season.

Cooked Grains

YIELD: 1½ CUPS

STEAMING METHOD

1 cup grain (rice, millet, fonio, or sorghum)

Fine salt to taste

TOASTED GRAIN METHOD

1 cup grain (rice, millet, fonio, or sorghum)

Fine salt to taste

1 tablespoon olive oil

Steaming Method

In a small pot, combine the grain with 2½ cups water. Season with salt and bring to a simmer over medium heat. Cook until the grains are just tender, 12 to 18 minutes. Cover and allow to sit until you are ready to serve. Just before serving, fluff with a fork.

Toasted Grain Method

In a small pot set over medium heat, pour in the grain and toast, swirling the pan constantly until the grain begins to crackle, becoming fragrant and deepening in color to a deep tan, about 10 minutes.

Turn the heat to low, carefully add in 1¼ cups water, season with salt, bring up to a simmer, and cook, partially covered, until the grain is cooked and softened, 12 to 18 minutes. Remove from the heat, drizzle in the olive oil, and let sit covered for at least 10 minutes. Fluff with a fork and allow to cool to room temperature. You can cook the grains ahead. Cool and store the cooked grains in the refrigerator for up to 3 days.

Ẹ̀wà sísè is a wonderful and simple side that works best with soft-skinned beans like ẹ̀wà olóyin (honey beans), black-eyed peas, yellow-eyed peas, or pinto beans. The onions become softened and lend their aromatic essence, melting into the body of the cooked beans as they are mashed in the pot.

Ẹ̀wà Sísè (Cooked Mashed Beans)

YIELD: 4 CUPS

2 cups dried ẹ̀wà olóyin or other dried beans (such as black-eyed peas, yellow-eyed peas, or pinto beans), soaked 4 to 12 hours

1 red onion, peeled, diced

Fine salt to taste

Drain out the soaking liquid and place the beans in a large pot. Add water to cover by 3 to 4 inches. Bring to a boil over high heat and lower to a simmer. Cook uncovered until the beans are tender and soft but not falling apart, about 50 minutes. Add more water if necessary to keep the beans from drying out. Add the onion, season with salt, and cook until the onions are softened, about 10 minutes. Allow the beans to cool slightly. Drain out any excess liquid by scooping out with a ladle.

Mash the beans to a coarse puree with the back of the ladle, a wooden spoon, or a potato masher.

Serve hot with Ata Dín Dín (page 93), with sides such as Dòdò (page 193), or with any of the boiled starches from pages 59–60.

BOILED OR STEAMED VEGETABLES

When talking about boiled starchy vegetables in Nigeria, there are two cooking methods we use: the submersion method, where it's fully submerged and cooked in a hot liquid, and steaming. In Nigerian English, the term "boiled" is used interchangeably to describe both techniques. Most of our root vegetables are commonly cooked using the submersion method, though they can also be steamed. Yams and cassava should be peeled before boiling, but plantains, sweet potatoes, and cocoyams (taro) can be cooked with the skin on.

Boiled Plantains

Green or yellow firm plantains with the skin on

Cut each plantain with the skin on, crosswise into 3- to 4-inch pieces. Place in a medium pot and pour in enough water to cover the bottom. Place the pot over medium heat, cover, and cook the plantains until tender and cooked though, about 15 minutes. Remove from heat and allow to cool enough to touch. Peel the skin off and serve the plantains warm, alongside Garden Egg Stew (page 122) or Ata Dín Dín (page 93).

Boiled Maize

Fresh whole corn in husk
Fine salt to taste

Remove the husk and silk from the corn. Cut each crosswise into 3- to 4-inch pieces. Place in a medium pot and pour in enough water to cover the bottom. Season with salt. Place the pot over medium heat, cover, and simmer the corn pieces until tender and cooked though, about 15 minutes. Remove from heat and allow it to cool enough to touch. Serve warm or room temperature alongside Èwà Sísè (opposite).

Boiled Yams

Whole yam tubers
Fine salt to taste

Fill a large bowl with water. Slice off the ends of the yam tuber and cut into 1½-inch-thick discs. Use a peeler or sharp knife to peel off the brown skin. Drop peeled pieces into the bowl of water as you peel to prevent the yam from oxidizing and browning. Once sliced and peeled, place in a medium pot and pour in enough water to cover the bottom. Season lightly with salt. Place the pot over medium heat, cover, and cook the yams until tender and cooked through, about 15 minutes. Remove from heat and allow it to cool enough to touch. Serve warm, alongside Stewed Sardines (page 123) or Garden Egg Stew (page 122), with palm oil or groundnut oil seasoned with a little salt.

NOTE A little bit of sugar can be added during the cook process to season the yams. This is typically done when the yams are freshly harvested and have not been aged. Aged yams tend to be a little sweeter as the starches begin to break down and are converted to sugars.

Boiled Cassava, Cocoyam, or Sweet Potato

Cassava, taro, or sweet potato roots, whole, skin on
Fine salt to taste

Fill a large bowl with water. Slice off the ends of the root tuber and use a peeler or sharp knife to peel off the brown skin. Drop peeled pieces into the bowl of water as you peel to prevent the root from oxidizing and browning. Cut the root into 3- to 4-inch pieces. Place in a medium pot and pour in enough water to cover the bottom. Season with salt. Place the pot over medium heat, cover, and cook the yams until tender and cooked though, about 15 minutes. Remove from heat and allow it to cool enough to touch. Serve warm, alongside Stewed Sardines (page 123) or Garden Egg Stew (page 122).

DRY ROASTED VEGETABLES

Corn, plantains, sweet potatoes, and yams are just a few of the vegetables served roadside, fresh off a grate that's been set atop hot coals. During the day, you'll see grilled vegetables and starches served as a snack with Soaked Garri (page 49) and dry roasted peanuts. It's a trio simply made in heaven! For me, side sauces are a must.

Although coal fire is among the primary methods of roasting veggies in Lagos, this recipe is written for the home oven. Peak season vegetables need very little seasoning. Dry heat is essential to preserving their flavors and adding a hint of smokiness.

The cook time for each vegetable will differ depending on its size. Except for skin-on plantains, vegetable pieces should be turned frequently for even color on all sides.

Roasted Plantains

Firm yellow plantains with the skin on.

Olive oil, for drizzling

Fine salt to taste

Black pepper to taste

Preheat the oven to 325°F.

Leaving the plantains whole, skin on, cut each plantain in half down the middle, lengthwise. Place the plantains on a baking sheet, cut side up. Drizzle with olive oil and season with salt and black pepper. Roast until the plantains are tender, and a skewer or knife inserted goes all the way through, about 40 minutes. Broil for 4 additional minutes to lightly brown the surface.

To serve, peel the roast plantains off the skin. Serve alongside Whole Roast Fish (page 165), Soaked Garri (page 49), and roast peanuts with some Ata Dín Dín (page 93) for dipping.

Roasted Maize

Fresh whole corn in husk

Preheat the broiler to high broil.

Remove the husk and silk from the corn. Place the corn pieces on a baking sheet and directly under the broiler. Roast, turning frequently, until corn is browned and charred in spots, evenly all around. Enjoy roast corn alone, or alongside any of the bean dishes starting on page 190.

Roasted Yam

Whole yam tubers
Canola oil, for tossing
Fine salt to taste

Preheat the oven to 425°F.

Fill a large bowl with water. Slice off the ends of the tuber and cut into 1-inch-thick discs. Use a peeler or sharp knife to peel off the brown skin. Drop peeled pieces into the bowl of water as you peel to prevent the yam from oxidizing and browning. Once sliced and peeled, cut each disc into ½-inch-wide matchsticks, continue to store in cold water. You should get about 5 or 6 sticks per disc.

Rinse and drain the yam pieces. Remove any excess water by spreading out on a paper towel to drain. Once dry, place the yam pieces on a baking sheet and toss with canola oil. Spread pieces in an even layer and season with salt.

Roast, turning occasionally, until tender and deep golden brown in spots, about 45 minutes. Serve fries warm with some Ọbẹ̀ Ata (page 171) or your favorite condiment on the side.

Roasted Cassava, Cocoyam, or Sweet Potato

Cassava, taro, or sweet potato roots, whole, skin on
¼ cup canola oil
Fine salt to taste

Preheat the oven to 425°F.

Fill a large bowl with water. Slice off the ends of the root tuber and use a peeler or sharp knife to peel off the brown skin. Drop peeled pieces into the bowl of water as you peel to prevent the root from oxidizing and browning. Cut the root crosswise into 3- to 4-inch pieces.

Rinse and drain the vegetable pieces. Remove any excess water by spreading out on a paper towel to drain. Once dry, place the pieces on a baking sheet and toss with the canola oil. Spread pieces in an even layer and season with salt.

Roast, turning occasionally, until tender and deep golden brown in spots, about 45 minutes. Serve fries warm with some Ata Dín Dín (page 93) or your favorite condiment on the side.

STEAMED AND WRAPPED IN LEAVES

This is a section of starches that are grated or blended into purees, seasoned, wrapped in leaves (banana here), and steamed. Each of these starches can be served alone or alongside a soup, a stew, or a condiment. Steaming imparts flavor when a starch is wrapped in a leaf and the resulting dish takes on the essence of the leaves. The most common leaves for steaming come from òle, a type of broad water lily leaf with a grassy, briny flavor. Banana leaves are also common and that's what I use throughout this book.

Wrapping starches in leaves is an art in Nigerian cuisine, and the kind of shape produced—from cylindrical to cone-shaped to triangular—can be an individual preference, or the hallmark of a particular region. Dishes such as èkọ tutu, ekuru, and mọ́ín mọ́ín are known for 3-D shaped cones. I've learned shaping a leaf into a sealed cone that holds a loose batter requires time and practice. Ekoki, ekpang nkukwo, and ayan ekpang are usually rolled into cylindrical shapes.

You can of course also pour any of these batters into large or single-serving casserole dishes for steaming. This method will save some time and you'll end up with similar results, save for the flavor from the leaves. These dishes are an excellent way to practice the technique.

This is a simple dish rooted in the cuisine of the Efik and Ibibio people of southeastern Nigeria. It features a grated yam, cassava or taro root steamed in òle or banana leaves. The resulting cooked starch is meant to be delicate, moist, and firm enough to slice with a fork. Ayang ekpang is a great place to start leaf-wrapping if it's new to you. It pairs well with a variety of flavorful dishes such as soups and stews, especially otong soup, and can be used as a swallow. Dishes such as these are also used as soft foods for weaning babies.

Ayang Ekpang Iwa

(Steamed, Grated Cassava)

YIELD: 6 PUDDINGS

2½ pounds cassava root (about 2 whole)	1 pack banana leaves, defrosted for wrapping and steaming
2 tablespoons vegetable oil or other neutral oil	Red palm oil (for brushing leaves)
½ teaspoon fine salt	Ata Dín Dín (page 93) or Ẹ́fọ́ Rírò (page 239)

NOTE: AYAN EKPANG IKPONG (COCOYAM IN BANANA LEAVES) Here, cocoyam is grated or pulsed coarsely in a food processor, wrapped in leaves, and steamed using the same method as above. The result is a similarly wonderful side or accompaniment to soups and stews.

Remove the brown skin on the cassava roots by peeling off with a paring knife. Put the peeled roots into a bowl of water to keep them from turning brown.

Using the fine side of a box grater, grate all the peeled cassava pieces into a bowl. You can do this with a food processor and pulse to get a coarsely chopped puree. Fold in the vegetable oil and salt.

Cut banana leaves into six 10 x 10-inch squares. Save any trimmings to line the pot. Wipe leaves clean with a damp towel. Place a tall stockpot or dutch oven on the stove and line the entire bottom with up to two layers of banana leaf trimmings. Pour 2 cups of water in the bottom of the pot, behind the leaf layer.

Lay a banana leaf square flat on your work surface. Brush with a light layer of red palm oil. Transfer ¼ cup of filling to the leaf along an edge with about 1 inch of room for folding over and a 2-inch gap on each end. Roll the closest end of the leaf over the filling, then tuck and roll firmly into a cylinder. Seal one end of the cylinder by folding back and upwards. Leave the other end open. Place the filled cone upright in the pot, sealed end down. Repeat this step until all the batter is used up and the filled cones are all upright in the pot. If there is too much room in the pot, use the scrap pieces of banana leaves to fill the extra space to keep the cones upright and sealed. Cover the top of the pot with several leaves and place lid on top.

Steam wraps until the puree is cooked through and firm, about 20 minutes. You can test for doneness by taking one out and unwrapping, there should be no raw batter and it should be set firm. Allow to sit in the pot, covered for 15 minutes to cool slightly. Transfer to a baking sheet or serving platter. Serve warm with ata dín dín or éfo rírò.

Èkọ tutu is the Yorùbá name for a fermented corn pudding steamed in a leaf and served with anything from breakfast dishes to midday stews. The resulting cooked pudding has a natural waxy sheen from the leaf, as well as an earthy, slightly grassy flavor. Pouring a loose batter into cone-shaped leaf forms can take some practice (see guide on page 227), but the batter can also be poured into ramekins and steamed until set.

Èkọ Tutu
(Steamed Fermented Corn Pudding)

SERVES 6 TO 8

2 packs banana leaves, defrosted

2 cups fresh ògi paste or powder (page 42)

Ata Dín Dín (page 93) or Ẹ̀fọ́ Rírò (page 239), for serving

Cut the banana leaves into ten 11- to 13- inch squares. Save any trimmings to line the pot. Wipe leaves clean with a damp towel. Place a large stockpot or dutch oven on the stove and line the entire bottom with two layers of banana leaf trimmings. Pour 2 cups of water in the bottom of the pot, behind the leaf layer.

Combine ògi paste or powder with 4 cups of water. Whisk vigorously to break up and dissolve the ògi into the water. Place the stockpot over medium-low low heat.

Working one square at a time, fold the left corner of the leaf in toward the center, creating a straight vertical line that lines up with the center of the leaf. With your finger holding the center in place, hold up the leaf and use your other hand to fold the right corner of the leaf over the left fold—now you should have a cone shape with a closed, pointy bottom and an open top. Tighten the cone by pulling the right edge over until the bottom is closed. Seal the bottom by folding 1½ inches of the pointy end back and upwards. Line any tears on the inside of the cone with little pieces of leaf trimming to seal further. Hold the cone in an upright position with your finger on the folded bottom to keep the bottom edge sealed.

Ladle in ⅓ cup of the batter, just enough to fill about half of the way. Place filled cone upright in the prepared stockpot, sealed side down, leaving the tops open and leaning the cones up against the edge of the pot and one another to keep them sealed. Repeat folding and filling step until all the puree is used up and the filled cones are all in the pot. Use the scrap pieces of leaves to fill any extra space and keep the cones upright and sealed. If using cups, line each with a thin strip of banana leaf, pressing in for a tight fit. Ladle in ⅓ cup of the batter and place the cup in the prepared pot. Cover the top of the pot with several leaves and place the lid on top.

Increase the heat to medium and steam the èkọ until firm, about 25 to 30 minutes. You can test for doneness by taking one out and unwrapping; the paste should be set firm. Allow the èkọ to sit in the pot, covered for 15 minutes to cool slightly. Transfer to a baking sheet or serving platter. Serve warm alongside Mọ́ín Mọ́ín (page 226) or Ekuru (page 70) or by itself with some ata dín dín or ẹ́fo rírò.

This is another preparation of grated or pureed starches (corn, cassava, or yam can be used), enhanced with seasonings, spices, and aromatic ingredients such as stockfish or crayfish. Portioned into leaves, then wrapped and steamed, ekoki is typically served on its own or with condiment sauces. It hails from the Southeast and is often associated with the cuisines of Calabar, Efik, and Ibibio people.

Ekoki (Steamed Maize Pudding)

SERVES 6

½ small onion, peeled and roughly chopped

1 Scotch bonnet pepper

2 tablespoons dried crayfish

4 cups fresh or frozen sweet corn kernels

1 tablespoon red palm oil

One 6-ounce fillet smoked mackerel, flesh flaked, skin and bones discarded

2 teaspoons fine salt

1 pack banana leaves, defrosted

In the bowl of a food processor, add the onion, Scotch bonnet pepper, and crayfish and pulse to chop coarsely. Add the corn and pulse to form a coarse puree. Move the puree to a mixing bowl and fold in the palm oil and mackerel to incorporate. Season with the salt.

Cut the banana leaves into six 10 x 10-inch squares. Save any trimmings to line the pot. Wipe the leaves clean with a damp towel. Place a tall stockpot or Dutch oven on the stove and line the entire bottom with up to two layers of banana leaf trimmings. Pour 2 cups of water in the bottom of the pot, behind the leaf layer.

Lay a banana leaf square flat on your work surface. Brush with a light layer of red palm oil. Transfer ¼ cup of filling to the leaf along an edge with about 1 inch of room for folding over and a 2-inch gap on each end. Roll the closest end of the leaf over the filling, then tuck and roll firmly into a cylinder. Seal one end of the cylinder by folding back and upwards. Leave the other end open. Place the filled cone upright in the pot, sealed end down. Repeat this filling and folding step until all the batter is used up and the filled cones are all upright in the pot. If there is too much room in the pot, use the scrap pieces of banana leaves to fill the extra space and to keep the cones upright and sealed. Cover the top of the pot with several leaves and place the lid on top.

Steam the wraps until the puree is cooked through and firm, about 20 minutes. You can test for doneness by taking one out, unwrapping and cutting through the middle. There should be no raw batter and the paste should be set firm. Allow the ekoki to sit in the pot, covered for 15 minutes to cool slightly. Transfer to a baking sheet or serving platter.

Serve warm with Ntuen Ekpang (fresh pepper sauce, see Note, page 102), Ata Dín Dín (page 93) or Èfó Rírò (page 239).

NOTE: EKOKI IWA This preparation uses cocoyam that is grated and seasoned. Once steamed, the pureed root is wonderfully springy and dense. You can also substitute the corn for two medium cassava roots about 2 pounds/949 grams total. Follow directions above for wrapping and steaming.

Ekuru is a ground and steamed bean pudding. In its simplest form, it is seasoned lightly, and is one of the least intensive dishes you'll come across in this book. In Yorùbá it is also known as ekuru funfun, which translates as "white steamed bean pudding." Ẹ̀wà olóyin will do well in this dish with its subtly sweet taste, but other bean varieties such as cowpeas, black-eyed peas, and adzuki beans are great substitutes. Serve ekuru alongside Ẹ̀kọ Tutu (page 66), with a bowl of Ẹ̀kọ (page 117), or simply with Ata Dín Dín (page 93).

Ekuru (Steamed Bean Paste)

SERVES 6

2 packs banana leaves, defrosted

2 cups honey beans, soaked and peeled, or 2½ cups bean flour

1 small yellow onion, peeled and diced

1 Scotch bonnet pepper, any color, stemmed

1¼ teaspoons fine salt, plus more to taste

½ cup unsalted melted Manshanu (page 96), or neutral oil such as grapeseed oil

2 tablespoons ground crayfish (optional)

1 cups Ata Dín Dín (page 93), for serving

Cut the banana leaves into ten 11- to 13-inch squares. Save any trimmings to line the pot. Wipe the leaves clean with a damp towel. Place a large stockpot or Dutch oven on the stove and line the entire bottom with up to two layers of banana leaf trimmings. Pour 2 cups of water in the bottom of the pot, behind the leaf layer.

Working in batches, transfer the peeled beans to a food processor or blender and puree with ½ cup to 1 cup water until smooth. (If using bean flour, simply stir it in the water.) Stir in the onion, Scotch bonnet pepper, and salt. Add the manshanu and crayfish, if using. Puree to the consistency of slightly coarse whipped hummus.

The batter should be thick enough to softly hold its shape.

Place the stockpot over medium-low heat.

If using leaves, roll a square into a cone:

To shape the banana leaves for filling, working one square at a time, fold the left corner of the leaf in towards the center, creating a straight vertical line that should line up with the center of the leaf. With your finger holding the center in place, hold up the leaf and use your other hand to fold the right corner of the leaf over the left fold—now you should have a cone shape with a closed, pointy bottom and an open top. Tighten the cone by pulling the right edge over until the bottom is closed. Fold about 1½ inches of the pointy bottom back and upwards, sealing the bottom of the cone completely. Line any tears on the inside of the cone with little pieces of leaf trimming to seal further. Hold the cone in an upright position with your finger on the folded bottom to keep the bottom edge sealed.

Ladle in ⅓ cup of the batter, just enough to fill about half of the way. Place the filled cone upright in the prepared stockpot, sealed side down, leaving the tops open and leaning the cones up against the edge of the pot and one another to keep them sealed. Repeat this folding and filling step until all the puree is used up and the filled cones are all upright in the pot. If there is too much room in the pot, use the scrap pieces of banana leaves to fill the extra space and to keep the cones upright and sealed. Cover the top of the pot with several leaves (no need to trim them if there's overhang) to keep the steam within the pot and place the lid on top.

Set the heat to medium and steam the ekuru until firm, about 25 to 30 minutes. You can test for doneness by taking one out, unwrapping, and cutting through the middle. There should be no loose, raw batter, and the ekuru should be set firm. Allow the cooked puddings to sit in the covered pot for 15 minutes off heat to set up a bit more and to cool slightly. Transfer the wrapped cones to a baking sheet or serving platter. Unwrap and serve warm, by itself or alongside ata dín dín.

NOTE: HOW TO PEEL DRIED BEANS Place the beans in a medium bowl and cover with up to 2 inches of room-temperature water. Soak the beans for 45 minutes to 1 hour or until plump and the peel comes right off when you rub a bean between your palms.

Discard the soaking liquid. Fill the bowl with more water, grab a handful of beans and, working in the water, rub the beans between your palms. The peels will come right off and float above the beans. (The extra water will help provide an area for the skins to collect away from the beans.) Holding back the beans with one hand, pour the water and the peels into a colander set inside the kitchen sink. Discard the peels. Again, fill the bowl with water to cover the beans by several inches, and then peel and drain. Repeat this step up to 4 more times until about 95 percent of the beans are peeled.

INGREDIENT PREP AND COOKING GUIDES

Our stocks and base sauces highlight the subtle and striking regional differences within Nigerian cuisine. The building blocks of two separate sauces can be nearly identical, but by emphasizing one ingredient and omitting another, you can change the texture and character of a dish and create entirely new flavor profiles.

Having base stocks and sauces on hand is a crucial step to building a Nigerian pantry. It helps me feel like a more efficient cook when I break the food prep into steps that can be done ahead of time. When I set out to write this cookbook, I didn't plan to include recipes that require hours of long and lengthy preparation, but the key is finding the right balance of time and freezer space.

My mother's pantry was informed by her work in test kitchens for the Lagos-based branches of multinational food companies, so my exposure to ingredients and the basic components of flavor were vast. Even though we lived in the city, our backyard was a well-tended, small-scale farm, not uncommon in a region of the world where so many hail from agrarian roots—even in urban hubs like Lagos. My family grew a variety of fruits and vegetables, and raised chickens, pigs, and catfish. We were connected to food in a way that I haven't been since I moved to the United States. This interweaving of food—through growing, tending, and preparing—into our daily fabric is not just characteristic to Lagosians or Nigerians, but a commonality among Africans.

I remember my first weeks in the United States, seeing chicken breasts on display in pre-arranged plastic and foam containers and thinking, "Where is the rest of the chicken?" I will never become inured to this, and the question frequently lingers in my mind on trips to the grocery stores here in New York, which have little to do with the experience of buying meats in Nigeria. Most of the world knows that meat doesn't come pre-butchered from a grocery store, and most of the world doesn't experience it that way.

Nigerian cuisine is highly sophisticated in that the preparation and technique involved in cooking extracts nutrition and flavor from an array of ingredients. Meat is always *just* one more ingredient—not a meal in itself—and its absence means a dish often works best without it.

This may contrast with what meat signifies for you in a dish, but for me it conjures a sense that the *whole* animal is considered in our process of cooking with meat. Skin-on, bone-in cooking allows for cartilage, fats, and marrows to commune in the pot for tastes and textures that cannot be achieved other ways.

SEAFOOD AND MEAT GUIDE

Although Nigerian meals often include some element of meat or seafood, the primary source of protein comes from grains, pulses, and vegetables. Meat portions are small compared to the rest of the meal, and it is rare that specific parts of the animal are used independently of the other parts. For example, a fish stew will typically contain all parts of the fish—head and tail included—and a chicken stew may include the chicken feet, heart, and gizzard. With larger animals such as cows, your stew or soup will contain an assortment of cuts, skin, and offal. Exceptions are dishes where the soup is known for using a specific cut from the animal such as suya (beef filets), nkwobi (cow hooves), or isi ewu (goat head).

The vast majority of cooks prepare most meats used in everyday dishes using a two- or three-part method: first boiling the meat with aromatics and seasoning before adding to a pot of stew. Occasionally, the meat is deep fried after boiling; cooking in oil this way is used as a preservative step. Adding preserved meats to stews such as ọbẹ̀ dín dín (see headnote, page 93) results in a longer shelf life without refrigeration.

Below is a general guide to cooking the assortment of meats that go into the soups and stews in the chapters ahead. Any of these can be prepared separately, cooled and refrigerated up to two days in advance. The meats can also be frozen after cooking and will keep for up to one month. Defrost in the refrigerator and then use as directed.

SEAFOOD PREP

Dried Fish Pieces (stockfish)

YIELD: 1½ CUPS (200 GRAMS)

250 grams dried stockfish pieces

Rinse off the dried fish pieces and place in a pot. Cover with water about 2 to 3 inches above the surface. Bring to a simmer over medium heat and cook for 20 minutes until the fish begins to rehydrate and soften. Drain out the water and replace with fresh water. Repeat this process, cooking and replacing the water until the fish is soft enough to break apart with a fork, about three times total—the fish should be completely submerged in the cooking liquid at all times to properly rehydrate.

Remove from the heat and allow the fish to cool in the cooking liquid. Once cool enough to handle, pick out the bones and flake the fish into 1-inch pieces. Store the softened fish pieces covered with fresh water in a sealed container and refrigerate for up to 48 hours until ready to use. Use as directed in the recipe.

Smoked Fish

YIELD: 1 CUP (150 GRAMS)

250 grams smoked fish such as shawa or smoked catfish

Pick off the fish skin and bones and discard. Flake the fish fillet into 1-inch pieces. Use as directed in the recipe.

Dried Crayfish

YIELD: ¼ TO ½ CUP (25 GRAMS)

25 grams small to large dried whole crayfish

If using large crayfish, pick off the heads and reserve them for stock or pulse in a food processor into a coarse ground to use as ground crayfish.

In a medium bowl, add the crayfish pieces and cover with 2 cups of hot water. Allow to soak for at least 10 minutes before use. Follow recipe instructions for when to add to the dish.

Meat and Offal Cooking Instructions

SERVES 4

1 pound
(500 grams) meat,
chicken, or offal

1 onion, chopped

1 red Scotch
bonnet pepper

2-inch piece
of ginger, thinly
sliced

1 garlic head, cut
in half crosswise

1 tablespoon
atare seeds

8 fresh thyme
sprigs

Fine salt to taste

Add the meat, chicken, or offal pieces to a large pot and cover with about 3 inches of water. Add the onion, Scotch bonnet pepper, ginger slices, garlic, atare seeds, and thyme. Season the pot generously with salt. Bring to a boil over high heat, reduce the heat to medium, and allow to simmer until the meat is completely cooked, adding more water as necessary to cover the pieces. The meat should be tender enough to be pierced easily with a fork but not falling apart. If cooking meat or chicken, strain the meat out and reserve the cooking liquid to use as stock. Discard the cooking liquid for offal. Add the cooked meat to your soup or stew as directed in the recipe.

If working ahead, store the meat once cooled in airtight containers for up to 3 days in the refrigerator or for up to a month in the freezer.

NOTE Oven roasting and deep frying are additional methods used to cook meats and are steps that can be done after the meat has been boiled. These methods mainly help extend the shelf life of your cooked meat before adding to a soup or stew. Meats are also roasted or fried when cooking large quantities for gatherings or parties where the pieces can sit at room temperature and quickly be tossed or dropped into ọbẹ̀ dín dín (see headnote, page 93) before serving.

STOCKS

In Nigerian cooking, it's rare to create a stock where the meat, seafood, or poultry is immediately discarded. They are used as ingredients to add flavor and typically end up in soups or stews. The cooking liquid becomes a base for a variety of dishes. This economical use of ingredients is typical in most Nigerian households. Watching my mom cook in Lagos is like taking a master class in "Food Waste Reduction." Every part of the ingredient seems to have a function— from providing nourishment to enriching the soil for her garden as compost. Back in Brooklyn, I make large pots of stock from meat or chicken bones from previous meals.

Below are my basic methods for preparing a meat or chicken stock and fish stock. Any of these will provide you with an infused flavorful liquid to add richness to the dishes in the chapters ahead.

Meat or Chicken Stock

YIELD: 2 QUARTS

1 pound (400–500 grams) bone-in beef, goat, lamb, or chicken, cut into 3- to 4-inch pieces, or meat or chicken bones

½ pound (200 grams) cut pieces of cow foot (optional)

2 large onions, quartered

2-inch piece of ginger, peeled and thinly sliced

1 head of garlic, halved

1 fresh bay leaf

6 to 8 fresh thyme sprigs

1 tablespoon atare seeds

1 Scotch bonnet pepper (optional)

2 ounces fresh lemongrass leaves or 2 fresh lemongrass stalks

1 bunch of fresh herbs, such as parsley, cilantro, or dill—whatever you have on hand will do here

In a large stockpot, combine the meat or chicken bones, cow foot pieces, if using, onion, ginger, garlic, bay leaf, thyme sprigs, and atare seeds. Pour in 8 cups water. Place the pot over high heat and bring the liquid to a boil. Reduce the heat to medium low and allow the stock to simmer until the meat is completely cooked and tender and the liquid is reduced by about a quarter of its original volume, 40 to 90 minutes. Skim off any foam from the surface as the stock reduces. If you are using meat pieces, you can remove them from the stock at this point once they are fully cooked and tender. Check for doneness at about 40 minutes for chicken and at 60 to 90 minutes for beef, lamb, pork, or goat.

If using bones, continue to cook and reduce the stock by following the instructions on the next page.

continued >

79

Ingredient Prep and Cooking Guides

Meat or Chicken Stock

< continued

Add the Scotch bonnet pepper, if using, lemongrass, and herbs. Press down to make sure the aromatics are submerged in the broth. Allow the stock to simmer for an additional 20 minutes to infuse it with the fresh herbs.

Line a colander with a layer of cheesecloth or a fine muslin cloth. Strain the stock through the colander and use as directed in your recipe or chill immediately. Store the stock for up to 3 days in the refrigerator or up to 1 month in the freezer.

Fish Stock

YIELD: 2 QUARTS

1 large whole fish, such as mackerel, croaker, bass, or snapper, cleaned and cut crosswise into steaks or 1 pound fish bones, including the head, tail, and fins

2 large yellow onions, quartered

2-inch piece of ginger, peeled and thinly sliced

1 head of garlic, halved

1 fresh bay leaf

6 to 8 fresh thyme sprigs

1 tablespoon atare seeds

1 red Scotch bonnet pepper (optional)

2 ounces fresh lemongrass leaves or 2 fresh lemongrass stalks

1 bunch of fresh herbs such as parsley, cilantro, or dill—whatever you have on hand will do here

In a large stockpot, combine the fish steaks (or fish carcass), onion, ginger, garlic, bay leaf, thyme sprigs, and atare seeds. Pour in 8 cups water. Place the pot over high heat and bring the liquid to a boil. Reduce the heat to medium low and allow the stock to simmer until the fish is cooked through, about 20 minutes. If using whole fish steaks, remove the fish pieces and set aside to use in any soup or stew. Continue to cook the broth, skimming off any foam from the surface as the stock reduces by a quarter. If using a fish carcass, keep the bones in as you reduce the stock.

Add the Scotch bonnet pepper, if using, lemongrass, and herbs. Press down to make sure the aromatics are submerged in the broth.

Allow the stock to simmer for an additional 20 minutes to infuse the fresh herbs.

Line a colander with a layer of cheesecloth or a fine muslin cloth. Strain the stock using a colander and use as directed in your recipe or chill immediately. Store the stock for up to 3 days in the refrigerator or up to 1 month in the freezer.

NOTE In addition to fish bones, your stock can also be made with dried or fresh shrimp shells, including the head and tails. Replace the fish steaks or fish bones with 1 pound of shrimp shells and follow the recipe as directed.

FOOD IS READY

Whether it's an invitation to the table or a handwritten sign announcing a roadside food stand, the phrase "food is ready" is used frequently in Nigeria to signal it's time to eat. The mouthwatering recipes that follow are classic versions of dishes you can expect to encounter all across Lagos. Cook through this book by using the following recipes as a guide and a source of inspiration.

CONDIMENTS, DRIED SPICE BLENDS, AND STARTER SAUCES

This section gives an overview of the essential condiments of Nigerian cuisine. The richness of our cuisine can come from even the smallest additions of flavor. Our condiments serve as multifaceted accents to rice, starches, vegetables, and meat. They can be easily prepared and kept refrigerated for days or weeks, and frozen for much longer. If you are looking for something simple to share with others, or for an introduction to the character and spice profiles of Nigerian cuisine, I recommend starting with these pantry staples. Perhaps you haven't had one of these dishes since childhood, or you have never made or seen one of these dishes before. These recipes aren't definitive, but they offer guidance on key ingredients and methods that will allow you to try out variations within your own cooking.

A WORD ON TECHNIQUE

The techniques that follow are as critical as the ingredients. Recipes are basically sets of instructions, and they serve us well when we need to make a very precise, exacting dish. But those types of instructions aren't as effective for guiding the creation of dishes that are built by layering flavors, dishes that demand attention to detail as much as to coloration, heat, timing, consistency, and texture. My hope is that these recipes serve as an introduction not simply to dishes but to the techniques that bring them alive. Indeed, they are what make our cuisine special! I describe noteworthy techniques below, and you'll find them in more detail throughout the book.

TOASTING SPICES

Toasting spices opens the dimensions of a spice's character. Spices are used in nearly all of the dishes in this book. Note that the process of blooming spices—toasting them in a hot pan, with or without oil—before adding them is most important when the dish is spice-forward. Toasting helps enhance and draw out aromas and flavor, and you'll notice the difference as you begin to make your own spice blends.

GRINDING SPICES

Purists will tell you that hand grinding spices is the technique that defines a dish, and that a grinding stone is the critical component to achieving *real* ata. As much as I love my high-tech kitchen tools, I am just as sentimental about our traditional approaches. But I simply do not have time to undertake hand grinding, and I doubt you do either. I recommend using a food processor or coffee grinder reserved just for spices to simplify this task.

CURDLING PALM OIL

This is a technique of combining palm oil and potash to create a rich and creamy sauce, perfect for adding a glossy finish to dishes such as nkwobi, abacha, and isi ewu.

BLEACHING PALM OIL

This technique works specifically to render red palm oil, which has a low-smoke point, more suitable to frying and other high-temperature applications. Raw, unfiltered palm oil is heated beyond its smoke point to neutralize both its flavor and color. This is not an industrial technique, but keep in mind that if done at home, it will almost certainly set off your smoke alarm. It's an important technique to feature as part of our essential repertoire, but not one that I employ often. For recipes that call for bleaching palm oil, African grocers will likely carry a store-bought version of smoked red palm oil.

FERMENTATION

Discussed in depth on page 39, fermentation is a valuable means of creating depth and complexity in our dishes. As an ancient food preservation technique, fermentation allowed for foods to keep longer in hot climates. It remains an important part of food preservation, especially when access to cold refrigerated storage is not guaranteed. But it also benefits digestion and nutrient absorption, and unlocks incredible dimensions of flavor. Note that for these recipes, fermentation can take up to twenty-four hours.

Ata gígé is a coarse puree of red bell peppers and onions, with Scotch bonnets for added heat and complexity. It is light, fresh, simple, and ready to be incorporated into your cooking. Ata gígé is ideal for condiment recipes like Ata Dín Dín (page 93) and Ofada Stew (page 220), where a coarse-ground base sauce lends colorful bits to a finished dish.

Ata Gígé

YIELD: 2 CUPS

2 medium red bell peppers, stemmed and seeded

1 medium red onion, roughly chopped

4 garlic cloves

1-inch piece of ginger, peeled and chopped

1 red Scotch bonnet pepper or 2 tablespoons Trinity Pepper Paste (page 102)

Working in batches if necessary, combine the bell peppers, onion, garlic, ginger, and Scotch bonnet peppers in a food processor or blender and pulse to a coarse puree. Ata gígé can be stored in a sealed container for up to a week in the refrigerator or up to a month in the freezer.

Ata lílọ̀ is a smooth puree of fresh pepper and tomatoes that serves as the base for several Nigerian dishes such as jollof rice and ọbẹ̀, a stew for cooked meats. This puree is added to a pan with oil and cooked; it is a wonderful accompanying sauce for drowning starches such as fùfú, steamed rice, yams, or plantains. It is almost identical to ata gígé in ingredient composition, but think of ata lílọ̀ as ideal for incorporating flavor into meats whenever low-heat, simmering, and braising techniques are used.

Ata Lílọ̀

YIELD: 2 CUPS

2 medium red bell peppers, stemmed and seeded

1 medium red onion, roughly chopped

One 14.5-ounce can peeled whole tomatoes

4 garlic cloves, peeled

1-inch piece of ginger, peeled and chopped

1 or 2 Scotch bonnet peppers, stemmed

Working in batches if necessary, combine the bell peppers, onion, tomatoes, garlic, ginger, and Scotch bonnet peppers in a food processor or blender and blend on high to a fine puree. The liquid from the can of tomatoes should suffice but you can add up to ¼ cup of water if necessary to get the puree going.

Ata lílọ̀ can be stored for up to a week in the refrigerator or for up to a month in the freezer.

NOTE Lagosians around Ebute Metta, Lagos Island, and the coast of Lagos serve fresh and uncooked ata lílọ̀ with roast fish. Abodo is a lightly roasted herring often served in this way.

A caramelized relish of onions, red bell peppers, and Scotch bonnet chiles cooked in a neutral oil until the flavors have melded, ata dín dín is my money sauce—the one I keep fresh and on hand 365 days of the year. Meant to last for several days in the refrigerator, it is best when it is reduced slowly, gently, and thoroughly; cooking out the moisture helps to preserve each ingredient. Whatever you mix with it turns into a fiery, subtly sweet, and deeply satisfying dish. Fried meats can be tossed in to create a dish called Ọbẹ̀ Dín Dín; it is the base for Garden Egg Stew (page 122) or Stewed Sardines (page 123); and it gives Ẹ̀fọ́ Rírò (page 239) its powerful complexity.

Ata Dín Dín (Buka Stew)

YIELD: 2 CUPS

2 cups Ata Gígé (page 89)

1 cup canola or other neutral oil such as grapeseed or safflower

Fine salt to taste

Pour the ata gígé into a shallow medium saucepan and bring to a simmer over medium heat. Cover and let simmer until the peppers and onions have softened, and released their liquid, 18 to 20 minutes. Pour in the oil and cook further, stirring frequently, until the sauce thickens and looks separated, about 15 minutes. Season with salt to taste.

This chile oil gives you a multilayered introduction to our cuisine. When I returned to New York from Lagos in early 2018, I brought bags and bags of chiles I'd been unable to find in the United States. I began making this oil to unleash the beautiful bouquets of our native chiles, and to add them to dishes I eat every day. Stored in an airtight jar, the oil will last refrigerated for a month at minimum. Typically served with Ẹ̀wà Agoyin (page 191), it works brilliantly with fish, seafood, meats, and roasted vegetables, usually as a finishing drizzle. While I've included substitutions, feel free to experiment with whatever variety of chiles you can find (especially those found in African markets). A neutral oil like grapeseed, safflower, or any vegetable oil will yield the best results.

Agoyin Sauce (Dried Chile Oil)

YIELD: 3 CUPS

8 ounces dried red chiles such as ancho or guajillo

4 ounces dried red chiles such as Thai or árbol

4 ounces dried tiny chiles such as bird's-eye

2 or 3 smoked, dried Cameroonian peppers or chipotle peppers

1 large red onion, chopped

6 garlic cloves

2-inch piece of ginger, peeled and chopped

2 cups neutral oil such as grapeseed, safflower, or canola

¼ cup dried crayfish, soaked in hot water

2 tablespoons irú (fermented locust bean), soaked in hot water

2 teaspoons fine sea salt

VARIATION To make a crispy variation, stir in ½ cup chopped raw peanuts and ¼ cup sesame seeds in the last minute of cooking. The nuts will toast beautifully and add a lovely crunch to the peppery chiles.

Clean the chiles and dried Cameroonian peppers, removing any stems and rinsing off any dirt. Snip any large chiles into 1-inch pieces using a pair of scissors and place in a large bowl. Pour in boiling water to cover and allow the dried peppers to soak until bloomed and rehydrated, 10 minutes.

Use a food processor or mortar and pestle to chop the onion, garlic, and ginger to a coarse paste.

Heat up a heavy-bottom medium-size saucepan over medium-low heat and add the oil and onion paste. Cook, stirring frequently until softened and fragrant, about 15 minutes.

Drain the chiles and peppers and working in batches if necessary, pulse into a coarse paste using the food processor or mortar and pestle. Add the chile paste to the cooked onion paste and stir to incorporate. Add the drained crayfish and drained irú and season with the salt. Cook over low heat, stirring frequently to prevent the sauce from burning, until all the moisture has cooked out, about 30 minutes.

Serve this oil over Ẹ̀wà Agoyin (page 191) or as a side dip for Whole Roast Fish (page 165). Store in an airtight container for up to a month in the refrigerator.

Unique to northern Nigeria and its neighboring regions, yaji commonly refers to a wide range of spice blends, most often used for meat seasoning and preservation. This blend reflects a common yaji component: roasted peanut powder, blended with spices and cayenne. Delicious, earthy, robust, and multilayered, many variations of yaji exist. Of course, the best spice blends in Lagos are found in the markets, usually upon the suggestions of locals and home cooks who know which version suits the dishes they want to make. No one spice blend recipe works for all possible uses, so please feel free to experiment—toasting the individual spices to different degrees will change each batch. Sprinkle yaji over Dan Wake (page 209), Masa (page 136), and Beef Suya (page 141).

Ground Yaji Spice Blend

YIELD: ¼ CUP

¼ cup dry roasted, peeled peanuts

1 teaspoon fine sea salt

1 tablespoon ground ginger

2 teaspoons ground cayenne

1 teaspoon garlic powder

Chop the peanuts in a food processor or work in batches using a spice grinder. Pulse just enough to grind into a coarse powder.

Transfer the peanut powder to a small bowl and add the salt, ginger, cayenne, and garlic powder; stir to incorporate.

Transfer the spice blend to an airtight container, cover, and store at room temperature.

NOTE Seasoning meat with this dried spice blend is a traditional means of preservation. There are other types of spice-preserved meats in Nigeria. Kilishi is a peppered and sun-dried jerky that's popular in the North and available in markets across Lagos. Another is dambun nama, a cut of spiced beef dried and shredded into thin threads, evocative of cotton strands.

Manshanu is a clarified fat made from fresh unpasteurized cow's milk. It is used in northern Nigerian cuisine to add creaminess and gloss to a variety of dishes. Its silky texture make it ideal for sautéing ingredients or finishing sauces. A locally made ingredient, manshanu is sometimes bulked up by combining it with raw animal fat. Pure clarified milk fat versions are available but more expensive. Since fresh unpasteurized cow's milk can be difficult to come by in Brooklyn, this recipe starts with a pound of butter and slightly browns the milk solids to give the butter a gentle, nutty fragrance. Manshanu, like other clarified butters such as ghee, has a high smoke point and will keep well for up to six months refrigerated. I use it generously in Móín Móín (page 226), to cook Sinasir (page 204), and to finish Dan Wake (page 209).

Manshanu

(Clarified Milk Fat)

YIELD: ABOUT ¼ CUP

1 pound unsalted butter

In a shallow saucepan, melt the butter over low heat. Cook until the milk solids separate and float above the fat. Skim off the milk solids using a slotted spoon. Continue to cook, stirring frequently until the moisture is cooked off and any solids that remain begin to brown slightly, about 10 minutes. Remove from the heat.

Cool slightly and pour the manshanu in a jar. Seal and store for up to 6 months in the refrigerator.

This blend of dried herbs and spices is named after my mother, Omotunde Rhoda Komolafe, who never travels without it. She sprinkles it on everything from eggs to chicken, and rubs it on whole fish and vegetables. It reminds me of her garden—an extraordinary plot of flowers, herbs, ferns, fruit trees, and leafy greens that surrounds the house. The care she takes in drying and milling these ingredients means you probably won't find anything like this in the markets of Lagos, but I want you to know it as closely as I do. Herbs and flower petals are crushed to give it a coarse consistency, which makes it ideal for both low- and medium-temperature baking and roasting, such as in Mom's Sunday Chicken (page 229).

Omotunde's Spice Blend

YIELD: 1 CUP

¼ cup dried crushed scent leaves or basil

¼ cup dried crushed edible flower petals, such as chive blossoms, rose petals, or any blossoms from herbs

2 tablespoons dried crushed mint leaves

2 tablespoons dried crushed wild oregano or marjoram leaves

In a large bowl, combine the scent leaves, flower petals, mint leaves, and oregano or marjoram leaves and toss with a spoon to incorporate. Store sealed in an airtight container at room temperature for up to 1 month.

I make this tamarind paste for drinks (page 268), for finishing dishes such as Kunu Gyada (page 243), and as condiments. Tamarind paste infuses everything it touches with a sharp, sour brightness. Markets and stores typically carry either tamarind pods or peeled tamarind pulp, which is usually a block of seedy, brown pulp wrapped in plastic. This recipe highlights an easy method of extracting tamarind's pulp from its seeds. The resulting paste should have the consistency of a thick puree. It will keep for at least a month in the refrigerator and freezes for longer.

Tamarind Paste

YIELD: 2 CUPS

450 grams whole tamarind pods or 300 grams tamarind seed pulp

If using whole tamarind pods, peel the tamarind shells and break up the pulpy seeds to loosen them. Discard the shells. If using pre-peeled pulp, break up the block with your fingers into a few pieces. In a small pot, cover the tamarind pulp with water and bring to a simmer over low heat. Stir and remove from heat. Allow to sit until cool enough to handle.

Use your fingers to loosen and separate the pulp from the seeds. The mixture will become a thick puree as you do this.

Set a fine sieve or cheesecloth set in a sieve over a large bowl and strain the tamarind puree. Press down on the sieve with a ladle or spatula to push the thick mixture through the sieve. Transfer the tamarind puree to a jar and discard the seeds and fiber.

This paste can be stored for at least a month in the refrigerator and longer in the freezer.

Peppersoup spice is a blend found across West Africa, and serves as the backbone for our many varieties of Peppersoup (page 175). Often a blend will be built around a dominant spice, and the specific components will vary according to the subregion where it's used. This version, inspired by spices commonly found in the southern Niger Delta region, has several central bases—the interplay of smoky uda peppers, uziza seeds, calabash nutmeg, and alligator peppers melds into a singular flavor experience. I've incorporated coriander and cumin to add some nontraditional complexity. Used generously in its namesake soup, this spice blend works brilliantly with fish and meat; it can be added to marinades and relishes when you want lingering heat and peppery notes to suffuse every ingredient with a little excitement.

Toasted Peppersoup Spice

YIELD: ¼ CUP

2 tablespoons grains of paradise (atare seeds)

4 uda pods, crushed open with the back of a knife

1 tablespoon uziza seeds

4 ehuru (calabash nutmeg) seeds, peeled

1 gbafilo seed, shell cracked into smaller pieces

2 teaspoons coriander seeds

2 teaspoons cumin seeds

Heat up a small skillet over medium heat and add the grains of paradise, uda pods, uziza seeds, calabash nutmeg seeds, gbafilo seed, coriander seeds, and cumin seeds. Toast, stirring frequently until the seeds begin to crackle and get fragrant, 4 to 5 minutes. Remove from heat and allow to cool enough to handle.

Transfer to a spice grinder and pulse to a smooth powder. Store away from heat or direct sunlight in an airtight jar until ready to use.

NOTE Ground peppersoup spice is widely available, and, like most of our dishes, the base spices vary by region and personal preference. The Niger Delta blends contain anywhere from eight to twelve components. The versions made by Igbo and Yorùbá cooks may contain fewer ingredients, but will feature delicately sweet calabash nutmeg and smoky selim peppers. It is difficult to say which spices are crucial and which can be omitted. I recommend picking out individual spices, toasting them, and making your own blend. Every time you make it, even the slightest alterations will lead to wonderful and surprising outcomes.

I use this spice blend generously in sweets and beverages such as Kunu Gyada (page 243) and Fura (page 45). Toasting the spices until each unique aroma emerges is a crucial step, and may require some trial and error.

Toasted Spice Blend for Sweets

YIELD: ¼ CUP

1 tablespoon shelled ehuru (calabash nutmeg) seeds

½ tablespoon whole grains of paradise (atare seeds)

2 teaspoons ground ginger

1 teaspoon chile powder

½ teaspoon grated nutmeg

1 teaspoon ground cinnamon

In a small pan set over medium heat, gently toast the ehuru seeds and atare seeds, stirring frequently in the pan until fragrant, 3 to 4 minutes. Allow to cool completely. Move to a grinder and pulse to a smooth powder. Add the ground ginger, chile powder, grated nutmeg, and ground cinnamon and pulse to combine. Move the mixture to an airtight container and store away from direct sunlight at room temperature until ready to use.

This relish of pounded fresh chile peppers highlights three fundamental flavor components of our cuisine: peppers, dried seafood, and fermented locust beans. Blending heat with complex umami flavors, it's a brilliant flavor enhancer for any sauces that may need extra spice or savoriness. It can also feature as a side condiment. This paste elevates dishes and evokes strong memories for anyone familiar with Nigerian cuisine.

Trinity Pepper Paste

YIELD: ½ CUP

1 cup yellow or red Scotch bonnet peppers

¼ cup crayfish, soaked in warm water and drained

1 teaspoon fresh or dried irú, soaked in warm water and drained

Working in batches if necessary, use a mortar and pestle to combine the Scotch bonnet peppers and crayfish. Pound to a coarse paste. Add the irú and pound further until incorporated to a smooth paste. Alternatively, do this step in a food processor and pulse to combine the ingredients until chopped.

Trinity pepper paste can be stored in an airtight container refrigerated for up to 1 week or frozen for up to 1 month.

NOTE Ntuen ekpang, also known as fresh pepper sauce, is a condiment of chopped fresh Scotch bonnet peppers. It's made without the crayfish and fermented locust beans and served alongside dishes such as Ekoki (page 69).

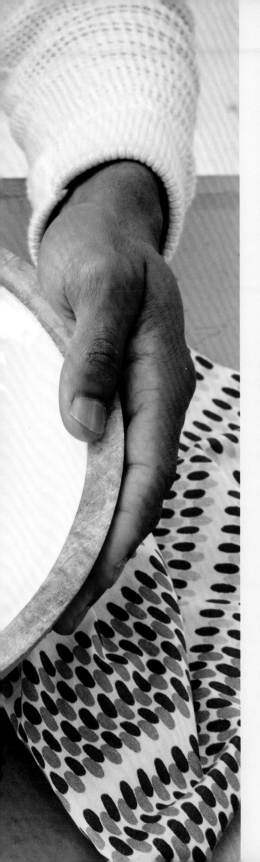

This recipe is as simple as it gets, with a base of red palm oil and potash. The potash thickens and stabilizes the red palm oil, resulting in a bold, creamy, bright orange sauce. Ucha is used in recipes such as Nkwobi (page 206) and Abacha (page 186). Grated ehuru accents this base sauce with deep woodsy notes. Use it as a dip for grilled fish or as a vinaigrette to drizzle over grilled vegetables. A splash of acid will only enhance its fragrant essence.

Ucha
(Creamy Red Palm Oil Sauce)

YIELD: 1 CUP

1 teaspoon
powdered kaun
or ¼ teaspoon
baking soda

1 cup red palm oil

1 to 2 tablespoons
Trinity Pepper
Paste (page 102)

½ teaspoon grated
ehuru (calabash
nutmeg)

1 teaspoon fine
salt, plus more
to taste

In a small bowl, combine the kaun with 2 tablespoons water and stir to dissolve.

Pour the palm oil into a large mixing bowl and whisk in the kaun mixture until the oil begins to thicken and curdle. Stir in the pepper paste and add the grated ehuru. Season with salt.

MEALS TO START YOUR DAY

The sun rises early in Lagos, and the temperature and humidity rise with it. Nigerian breakfast foods, equal parts nourishing and nurturing, provide a genius sense of balance. The dishes may be the least flavorful yet most filling of our offerings because they have a distinct purpose: to fuel you for the hard day's work that lies ahead. Lagos is no different from other African cities in the way its streets fill at daybreak with vendors on foot, in kiosks and bukas peddling dense, handheld bites and cups of hot tea to wash them down. Our breakfasts are typically carb-heavy and designed to keep you satiated and sustained as you venture out into the vibrant day and sweltering heat.

Think of the recipes here as first meals for breaking fast, but they are by no means foods eaten exclusively in the morning. Similar dishes are consumed across West Africa: corn is made into porridges, beans show up as fritters, grains are fermented, and imported goods such as tinned fish and corned beef accent base sauces and stews.

These recipes are mainly about technique; each has a style of preparation that distinguishes it from familiar breakfast foods in other parts of the world.

Ògi is, after all, just a corn porridge, but the fermentation process and ease of preparation are what makes it special. You'll encounter typical egg-and-bread dishes, but pungent spice or sauces accompany them. Dishes of dairy and grains that may be familiar to non-Nigerian readers are augmented by the sweet tang of fermentation or unique pairings, like fritters in porridge. Tradition suffuses so many of these breakfast staples. Though the influences of the Portuguese and British are evident in some dishes—such as fluffy bread made with refined, processed white flour—the origins of others stretch back centuries to indigenous foodways. Our ancestral diets centered whole foods, embraced seasonality, and honored the variety of the ingredients available. They also happen to be heavily plant-based, and gluten-free.

Nigerian foodways are the result of a careful understanding of the earth and a sacred recognition of what the earth can provide. It is no wonder that traditional ceremonies celebrating the harvest of various indigenous crops continue even today. In our culinary traditions, each ingredient is considered carefully and understood for the complexity of flavor and nourishment it yields. There is nuance to what we choose. For us, yam is not just yam: but either fresh yam, aged yam, or fermented yam. Those distinctions are crucial because that yields a difference in preparation. We have an appreciation for the ingredients that thrive in our climate: we preserve them through the seasons and find a myriad of uses for them from culinary to medicinal and ceremonial.

While I typically prefer unsweetened herbal teas, a cup of milky black tea always brings on a wave of nostalgia. Nigerians of a certain age will refer to almost any steaming hot beverage as "tea"—even warm chocolate milk. The tea culture I knew in Lagos was rather austere. We used no infused spices, had no grand traditional ceremonies or elaborate vessels to catch your eye. Still, breakfast was usually washed down with a hot cup of tea. You won't need a lot of ingredients here, just a few lumps of sugar, a splash of milk, and your favorite mug.

Milky Black Tea

SERVES 4

¼ cup black tea leaves or 4 black tea bags

Sweetener such as sugar or honey, to taste

Warm milk or evaporated milk, to taste

Heat 4 cups of water in a saucepan over medium heat. Bring to a boil and add the tea leaves or bags once simmering. Remove from the heat, cover, and allow to steep anywhere from 1 to 4 minutes, depending on the strength you prefer. Strain the tea into cups. Serve hot with a sweetener and lots of warm milk.

NOTE Tea can also refer to a milky hot chocolate drink, usually warm and made with malted chocolate drink powders.

I practically lived on this milk during my visit to Lagos in February 2020. I spent most of my days in traffic, crawling from vendor to market to restaurant, and, finally, to an auntie's house (or two). I packed a cooler in the backseat of the car with a bottle of kunun aya, ready for whenever I felt a rush of hunger coming on.

Tigernuts are tiny nut-like tubers that taste like a cross between pecans and almonds. They are grown across Africa, and in Nigeria, they're cultivated in the North and can be found at the market in nearly all forms: fresh, dehydrated, roasted, or milled into a flour. On their own, they're delicious—mild, slightly sweet, and nutritious—full of protein, calcium, magnesium, and fiber. When rehydrated and pressed, these tiny tubers yield a thick and creamy liquid. An important step in extracting the milk is allowing the nuts to soak for at least 12 hours, a process I refer to here as "blooming." I'm always surprised at how much liquid tigernuts can absorb. They plump up after a good soak—about 2 to 3 times their original size.

Kunun aya is typically served sweetened with crushed dates or honey and spiced with ginger. This filling beverage can be enjoyed at room temperature or chilled, and will keep for up to 3 days in the refrigerator, and up to 3 months frozen.

Kunun Aya (Tigernut Milk)

SERVES 4

2 cups (330 grams) whole, dried tigernuts

½ cup (50 grams) pitted medjool dates, halved and soaked in warm water

1 teaspoon Toasted Spice Blend for Sweets (page 101)

½ teaspoon fine salt

Place the tigernuts in a large bowl and cover with water about 4 inches above the top of the tigernuts. Cover the bowl with a kitchen towel and let stand at room temperature for at least 12 hours and up to 24 hours.

Drain off the soaking liquid and discard. Puree the soaked tigernuts and the dates in a high-speed blender with 4 cups warm water until very smooth. Do this in batches if necessary.

Strain into a bowl over a fine-mesh sieve or a muslin cloth and discard the tigernut pulp. Stir the toasted spice blend and salt into the milk. Transfer to a bottle or airtight container. It will keep for up to 48 hours refrigerated and up to a month frozen.

Over the course of the nearly two decades that I was unable to visit Nigeria, I was fortunate enough to have my parents visit at least once a year. During my college years, we occasionally stayed together in hotel rooms. Once I could afford to share an apartment with my brother Seeni, we would host them and attempt to rekindle some sense of Lagosian tranquility through cooking together.

My mom would typically make breakfast: a skillet full of decadent and tomatoey Naija eggs served with thick slices of yam or whatever sweet American white bread we could find that most closely resembled Agége Bread (page 115). The scent of her dried herb seasoning blend (page 97), mixed and packed right before her trip, would hang in the air as she cooked. In those moments, I knew that even if I couldn't visit home, a weekend tradition of home had come to me.

Jammy Tomato Breakfast Eggs

SERVES 4

1 tablespoon grapeseed or olive oil

1 small red onion, peeled and chopped

2 garlic cloves, peeled and sliced

1 12-ounce jar roasted red peppers, drained and chopped

1 fresh bay leaf

1 Scotch bonnet pepper or 1 teaspoon red pepper flakes

1 teaspoon fine salt, plus more to taste

1 14.5-ounce can whole peeled tomatoes

4 eggs, whole

2 teaspoons Omotunde's Spice Blend (page 97)

Pour in the oil and add in the onions and garlic. Cook, stirring often until softened, about 2 minutes. Stir in the chopped roasted red peppers, bay leaf and drop in the whole Scotch bonnet pepper or red pepper flakes. Season to taste with salt. Stir to incorporate and cook until the liquid from the roasted peppers evaporates, about 2 minutes.

Add in the whole peeled tomatoes plus liquid. Use the spatula to break the tomatoes open in the skillet. Rinse out the tin with 1 cup of water and pour the liquid into the skillet.

Increase the heat to high and bring the sauce to a simmer. Allow the sauce to reduce, stirring occasionally until thickened and about three-fourths of the original volume, 5 minutes.

Remove and discard the bay leaf and Scotch bonnet. Gently crack the eggs in one at a time and spaced out over the sauce. Cover with a lid or strip of aluminum foil. Cook until the whites of the eggs are set and the yolks runny, 6 to 8 minutes. Garnish the eggs with Omotunde's spice blend. Remove the skillet from the heat. Serve immediately along-side Agége Bread (page 115) or yam or plantain swallow (page 52).

A market classic that can be tricky to replicate at home, agége bread is a sweet, soft, dense white bread made from a rich dough. Named after a neighborhood in mainland Lagos where it was traditionally baked, it is an irresistible breakfast staple.

The dough will take its sweet time to rise. Make it up to a day ahead and allow it to slowly proof in the refrigerator (it will develop more flavor this way). The dough typically gets its pillowy texture from margarine, a vegetable oil-based spread that is folded in. I use unsalted butter for flavor here and add an egg to the dough.

This recipe requires a springform pan and makes a substantial pull-apart loaf. Serve warm, alongside Jammy Tomato Breakfast Eggs (page 112), Stewed Sardines (page 123), or a healthy slathering of additional butter. Don't forget milk tea for dunking!

Agége Bread

YIELD: MAKES ONE 9-INCH PULL-APART LOAF, ENOUGH FOR 8 TO 10 SERVINGS

1 cup (235 milliliters) warm water or milk (110°F)

1 tablespoon (10 grams) active dry yeast

¼ cup (60 grams) granulated sugar

3½ cups all-purpose flour (520 grams) plus more for flouring the work surface if necessary

¼ cup (38 grams) nonfat dry milk powder

1 teaspoon Toasted Spice Blend for Sweets (page 101, optional)

1 teaspoon (4 grams) kosher salt

1 large egg, lightly beaten

5 tablespoons (56 grams) unsalted butter, softened, divided

1 tablespoon honey

In the bowl of a stand mixer fitted with a dough hook, add the warm water, yeast, and granulated sugar. Let stand, undisturbed, until foamy, 8 to 12 minutes.

In a separate bowl, whisk together the flour, milk powder, spices, and salt. Once the yeast is foamy, add the egg and the flour mixture to the bowl of the stand mixer. Stir with a wooden spoon just until a shaggy dough forms and add 3 tablespoons of softened butter.

With the mixer on low, knead the dough until it comes together into a stiff but stretchy dough, about 12 minutes. Shape into a smooth ball, place in a large, clean bowl, and cover the bowl with a kitchen towel. Let stand until doubled in size, 1 to 1½ hours.

Use 1 tablespoon butter to grease the sides and bottom of a 9-inch-wide, 3-inch-deep round springform pan.

In a small bowl, combine the last tablespoon of butter and the honey. Stir together until smooth. Set aside.

Punch the dough down to deflate and turn out onto a lightly floured work surface.

continued >

Agége Bread

< continued

Use a bench scraper to cut the dough into 16 even-sized pieces (about 56 grams each). Shape each piece into round balls by rolling tightly on your kitchen surface or a wooden board. Transfer each dough piece, seam side down to the buttered pan. Start with a piece in the middle, and then place the remaining pieces in a concentric circle around the center. Cover the pan with a clean dish towel and allow the dough to rise again until it is just below the top edge of the pan, about 45 minutes, depending on the temperature of your kitchen.

While the dough completes this last rise, preheat the oven to 325°F. Slide an oven rack on the very bottom rung of your oven and slide a baking sheet in.

Move the springform pan to the oven. Pour 2 cups of water in the baking sheet to create some steam. Bake the bread until the top is a light golden brown and the loaf sounds hollow when the surface is tapped, about 50 minutes. An instant-read thermometer should read 190°F when inserted in the center of the loaf.

Remove the loaf from the oven and transfer to a wire rack, allowing the bread to cool slightly in the pan, about 15 minutes. Unmold the sides of the pan and brush the surface with the honey butter mixture. Move the loaf to a rack to cool completely. Serve as nice 1-inch-thick slices, buttered and toasted for breakfast or alongside some warm milk tea for dunking!

Baked bread can be stored for up to 2 weeks in the freezer.

DO AHEAD The dough can be made up to a day ahead, sealed in a resealable plastic bag and slowly proofed in the refrigerator overnight. To bake, remove from the refrigerator and let sit to remove the chill, about 30 minutes. Shape, place in the pan, and proceed with the steps that follow.

In Yorùbá, a bowl of cooked porridge made from fermented cornstarch is referred to as ẹ̀kọ or ògì. To the Yorùbá speakers in the hinterlands, ògì is the raw ingredient itself, and ẹ̀kọ the cooked result.

Ògì is usually found as a fresh paste at the markets in Lagos, dished out of large basins and sold by weight. It can be found as a dehydrated powder in sealed bags in grocery stores and online. For me, making the fermented paste from scratch is quite literally a labor of love; the cooked porridge itself is the last step for me—a quick and effortless one.

Once cooked, the porridge's flavors and aroma blossom. The slightly sour tang of hot ẹ̀kọ, sweetened with a dribble of honey, perfectly complements the fluffy earthiness of just-fried Àkàrà (page 219) or steamed Mọ́ín Mọ́ín (page 226). With àkàrà for dipping, this is a full meal to start your day—and you won't even need a spoon.

Ẹ̀kọ (Fermented Cornstarch Porridge)

SERVES 4

¾ cups ògì paste (page 42) or 1½ cups dry ògì powder

Fine salt, to taste

A sweetener such as sugar, honey or maple syrup to taste

Coconut milk, coconut cream, or any nut milk, for serving (optional)

Warm Àkàrà (page 219) or Mọ́ín Mọ́ín (page 226), for serving

In a medium pot, combine the ògì paste (or powder) with 3 cups of water and whisk to dissolve completely. Cook the mixture over low heat, stirring constantly until it thickens and becomes opaque with bubbles slowly rising to the surface, 8 to 10 minutes.

Remove from the heat and stir in the salt. Carefully ladle the hot porridge into bowls. Top with a spoonful of sweetener and a splash of coconut milk or cream, if using. Serve hot, alone or with warm àkàrà or mọ́ín mọ́ín.

NOTE: KOKO A northern Nigerian dish known as Koko in Hausa is a spiced fermented porridge, served warm and fragrant with hints of nutmeg, smoky selim seeds, ginger, and a touch of dried chile powder.

Koko also refers to a version of ẹ̀kọ made by the Awe people of Oyo state where the ògì paste is shaped into tiny balls and dropped into a loose, cooked porridge. The resulting porridge is thickened and lumpy with dumpling-like mounds in a soupy base.

Meals to Start Your Day

Fermenting grains enhances their nutritional benefits, makes them easier to digest, and shortens their overall cook time. You can ferment grains for up to 12 hours at room temperature. Any longer than 12 hours, the grains should be refrigerated and allowed to slowly ferment cold.

Fermenting grains is a step to be completed ahead of time. A variety of unprocessed grains including white and brown rice, millet, sorghum, and fonio can be used. Treat the cooked grains as you would a blank canvas: this bowl can be topped with any fruit or vegetable that's on hand or in season.

Sprinkled with sea salt and spiced nuts, these grain bowls are balanced and filling. My favorites run the gamut from sweet to savory: a spoon from a jar of last summer's fruit compote, pickled vegetables, honey, toasted coconut, or even a soft-boiled egg. When fermented just right, the grains remain the star of the dish.

Fermented Grain Bowl

SERVES 2 TO 4

1 cup short grain white or brown rice, millet, or sorghum

Fine salt to taste

Sweet toppings: fresh fruit, dates, honey, coconut milk or any nut milk, cream

Savory toppings: blanched or stir-fried greens, soft-boiled eggs

Crunchy toppings: benne seeds, toasted nuts such as peanuts or cashews

Place your rice, millet, or other grain in a bowl and cover with about 2 inches of water. Cover the bowl with a dish towel and allow to soak and ferment slightly for up to 12 hours at room temperature.

When ready to cook, bring 2 cups of water to a simmer in a medium saucepan over medium heat and sprinkle in some salt. Drain the water from the bowl of soaked grains and add the grains to the simmering water. Allow to cook and soften slowly over low heat, stirring occasionally, until all the water is absorbed and the grains are tender, 15 to 20 minutes. Cover and remove from heat. Allow to sit for at least 10 minutes. Loosen into large clumps by fluffing with a fork. Divide into shallow bowls and serve with any of the toppings you desire.

This homemade yogurt is more of a project than a recipe. Growing up curious about food and with a food scientist mother meant making this would quite literally be our fun Saturday together. Making yogurt like this could be intensely interactive, involving everything from carefully observing the milk for its change in consistency to draining and pressing to ensure the right thickness.

We never used thermometers or timed our steps, so this recipe is more a standardization of my approach than the singular and essential method for making yogurt at home. I recommend to everyone new to homemade yogurt-making to use a thermometer to determine when the correct temperatures are achieved, and with practice, you'll be able to do this by observation alone.

Homemade Yogurt

YIELD: 1 QUART

4 cups whole milk
½ cup heavy cream

4 tablespoons plain whole milk yogurt with live active cultures

Combine the milk and cream in a pot and set over low heat. Warm until it is just beginning to simmer around the edges and steam rises from the surface (180° to 200°F). Transfer the mixture to a bowl and allow to cool down until warm to the touch (110° to 118°F). Whisk the live yogurt cultures into the milk. Cover with a towel and move to a warm spot in your kitchen. The oven (turned off, with the light on)

works great for this. Let it sit for 6 to 12 hours; the longer it sits, the more sour it'll become.

If you want a thicker and creamier yogurt, line a colander with cheesecloth and set it over a bowl. Transfer the yogurt to the cheesecloth, cover with a piece of plastic, and let the whey drain out for 8 to 12 hours in the refrigerator.

I'm not a morning person, but the promise of garden eggs stewed in a tomato-based sauce never fails to get me to the breakfast table. Garden eggs, as they are called in Nigeria, are tennis ball-sized varieties of the nightshade family. They come in shades of green, yellow, orange, or white and look like baby eggplants.

With a slightly bitter taste, they can be eaten fresh, or simmered gently in a stew. They are found almost year-round in Lagos. In Brooklyn, I've come across the occasional fresh garden egg at produce stands on Church Avenue in East Flatbush, where a community of West African and Caribbean immigrants first began settling in the 1970s and '80s. Adequate garden egg substitutes are baby eggplants or a whole eggplant, diced into cubes.

Serve this stew over any steamed starch such as plantains, yam, potatoes, or cassava.

Garden Egg Stew

SERVES 4 TO 6

3 tablespoons neutral oil such as grapeseed or canola

6 medium garden eggs (or any color baby eggplants, about 2 pounds total), trimmed and cut in half or quarters if large

1 cup Ata Dín Dín (page 93)

1 teaspoon fine salt, plus more to taste

4 loose cups spinach leaves, chopped kale, mustard greens, beet greens or turnip greens

¼ cup sliced scallions

¼ cup fresh dill fronds, chopped

Steamed yam, plantain, or sweet potato slices, for serving

In a large skillet over medium heat, add 1 tablespoon of oil and heat till it shimmers. Working in batches if necessary, place the garden eggs in the skillet cut side down. Sear the contact side to a deep golden brown, about 3 to 5 minutes. Move to a plate and repeat the browning with an additional tablespoon of oil and the remaining garden eggs.

Wipe out the skillet with a paper towel. Pour in another tablespoon of oil and heat it over medium heat. Add the ata dín dín and cook until any liquid reduces and the sauce becomes jammy, 8 minutes.

Return the browned garden eggs to the skillet, nestling each piece seared side up in the sauce till almost submerged. Season the sauce with salt. Cook until the garden eggs are just soft with little resistance when poked with a fork, 2 to 3 minutes.

Add the greens, stir, and heat just enough to wilt the leaves. Remove the skillet from the heat. Garnish with the scallions and dill. Serve immediately with a steamed starch.

The company behind the Titus brand of tinned fish were genius marketers. They had so cornered the Lagos market that when I was growing up, I had no idea that sardines could be sourced fresh. I had this revelation years later while helping to process a huge order of fresh sardines for the dinner menu at the now-closed Brasserie Tatin in Baltimore.

Though you are free to use fresh sardines (and you won't regret the results), this recipe is a product of my nostalgia. I've felt unbridled joy in finding these sparkly, little red tins at African grocers or peeking out of my mother's suitcases during visits. A little ata dín dín, some freshly chopped tomato, a tin of sardines, and lots of fresh herbs combine to make a savory, salty, umami-rich delight. Serve alongside boiled yams, plantains, or another starch for a satisfying breakfast or quick lunch.

Stewed Sardines

SERVES 4 TO 6

1 tablespoon neutral oil such as grapeseed or canola

1 cup Ata Dín Dín (page 93)

Fine salt to taste

2 tins sardines packed in oil, drained, or 8 whole fresh sardines, heads and tails on, cleaned

1 large tomato, sliced into wedges

½ cup cilantro leaves and tender stems

¼ cup fresh dill fronds, chopped

Boiled yam slices or plantains (pages 59 and 60) or Agége Bread (page 115), for serving

1 lime, cut into wedges, for serving

In a medium saucepan, heat the oil over medium heat. Add the ata dín dín and cook until any liquid reduces and the sauce becomes jammy, 8 minutes. Add the sardines and tomato wedges and cook over low heat until the fish is warmed through, 6 minutes. If using fresh sardines, cook until they are cooked through, turning the fish once through the cooking process, 8 minutes.

Remove from the heat and garnish with the fresh cilantro and dill. Serve alongside boiled yam or plantains or thick slices of agége bread, with lime wedges for squeezing.

SMALL CHOPS AND STREET FOOD

All of the important textures of Nigerian cuisine—from the juicy crisp of our dòdò, to the slippery smoothness of our ogbono—can be found in our street food culture. What Nigerians call "small chops" are bite-size snacks, brought alive with accompaniments or sauces. They can be eaten on the go, accompany other courses, or start any meal.

With these dishes, we require no seating, no table settings, and no illustrious ceremony. You do not need to bow to a wide bowl or carefully dive into what is piled high on a platter. These small bites are simple and straightforward, meant to be consumed quickly. No Nigerian get-together is complete without small chops.

Although small chops are simple to prepare, they carry an unexpected complexity. They excite the palate by awakening it from between-meal dormancy with their all-encompassing flavor profiles.

They require techniques that we employ regularly—spice blending, marinating, frying, open-air grilling, fire roasting, and fermenting. Dishes from this chapter, such as peppered meats and òjòjò, serve as valuable introductions to Nigerian cuisine. A word to the wise: it's only with patience and careful attention to detail that a small chop's flavors reveal themselves.

This is a quick and easy snack. Groundnuts are slightly salty, earthy, and mildly sweet on their own. Here, their flavor is accentuated by the addition of Ground Yaji Spice Blend (page 95). This is a great way to enjoy just-harvested peanuts if you have access to them.

Boiled Groundnuts
WITH YAJI SPICE

SERVES 4

Sea salt

1 pound raw whole (shell-on) peanuts

Ground Yaji Spice Blend (page 95) or Toasted Peppersoup Spice (page 99), for serving

Bring a large pot of heavily salted water to a boil over medium-high heat. Add the peanuts, and turn down the heat to a simmer. Allow to cook until nuts are softened and crush easily when pressed out of their shells, about 45 minutes. Check for this by breaking the nuts out of one shell and crushing with your fingers. Remove the pot from the heat and allow the nuts to cool slightly in the cooking liquid, about 30 minutes.

Serve the boiled groundnuts drained and dusted with spoonfuls of yaji spice blend.

Cooked yams or a leftover pot of Àsáró (page 153) can be repurposed as yam fritters to serve as a small chop. This recipe is as easy as it gets, made both rich and refreshing by the addition of Ata Dín Dín (page 93) and fresh scallions. The garri-dusted crust is my recommendation, but you can also use breadcrumbs or panko for this step. Serve warm or at room temperature with extra ata dín dín for dipping.

Crushed Yam Fritters

SERVES 8 TO 10

2 pounds yam (about 1 whole yam)

1 teaspoon fine salt, plus more to taste

1 cup Ata Dín Dín (page 93), plus more for serving

¼ cup minced green onions or scallions

1 tablespoon grated ginger

3 eggs

2 cups cornstarch

2 cups garri or panko bread crumbs

4 cups vegetable or other neutral oil such as grapeseed, sunflower, or canola oil, for frying

Prepare two baking sheet by lining one with a sheet of parchment paper and placing a cooling rack inside the other.

Cut the yam into thick 1½-inch slices. Remove the brown skin on the slices by peeling off with a paring knife or a vegetable peeler. Put the peeled pieces into a bowl of water to keep them from turning brown.

Rinse off the yam pieces and place in a medium saucepan. Cover with water and bring to a boil over medium-high heat. Season with salt and reduce heat to a simmer. Allow the yam to cook until softened, about 10 minutes. Drain off any remaining liquid and move the yam to a bowl. Mash the yam into a chunky paste with a fork or potato masher and allow to cool completely.

Add the ata dín dín, green onions, and ginger, stir to incorporate. Season the mix with 1 teaspoon salt. Gently whisk 1 egg and fold it into the yam mixture. Scoop the mixture into tablespoon-size balls using an ice cream scoop or a tablespoon measure and place on the prepared baking sheet. Refrigerate until the scoops are chilled through, at least 1 hour. At this point the scooped balls can also be frozen by placing the baking sheet in the freezer. Once frozen, store the scooped mix in an airtight container or bag for up to 2 weeks.

Prepare a dredging station using 3 separate medium-sized containers, and adding the remaining 2 eggs, the cornstarch, and garri or panko. Lightly beat the eggs and season each bowl lightly with salt. Heat the oil in a medium saucepan to 325°F or until a drop of water sizzles when sprinkled in.

Dip the yam balls in the cornstarch first, then the egg mixture, then coat with the garri, panko or breadcrumbs. Fry the dipped yam balls until golden brown and warm all the way through, 4 to 6 minutes. Turn frequently to ensure an even color all around. Set the fritters on a rack inserted in the baking sheet to drain.

Serve warm with additional ata dín dín for dipping.

Every time I return to Lagos, I experience a rush of sensations: I am stimulated and nostalgic by what I see and experience. On each visit, I try to fit in a mid-week family road trip for a short break from the energy of Lagos. On my first trip back in twenty years, my family and I drove to Ibadan in Oyo state, the third largest city in Nigeria and just a few hours northeast of Lagos. A major interstate highway connects the two cities, and at each town we passed, the roadway was lined with street vendors.

Ìkírè is a town near Ibadan known for this namesake plantain dish. Very ripe and soft plantains are diced and fried, traditionally in red palm oil, until the pieces form a deeply caramelized, almost burnt crust. The dòdò is tossed with crushed chile and red onions while still hot, resulting in a snack that is at once sweet, slightly bitter, and peppery. Traditionally served wrapped in banana or plantain leaf, or sold roadside packed in small, cone-shaped plastic bags, this snack is a tangible way for me to relate what being back home in 2018 felt like—a rush of bittersweet and contrasting emotions.

Dòdò Ìkírè

SERVES 4 TO 6

4 ripe medium plantains (about 2¼ pounds)—mostly black plantains, soft with some yellow spots

Palm oil, for frying

1 small red onion, minced

1 teaspoon ground ginger powder

1 bird's-eye chile, chopped, or ½ teaspoon red pepper flakes

Fine salt to taste

Peel the plantains by using a sharp knife to make a slit in the skin down the length of each plantain, being careful to not cut the flesh, and remove the skin by peeling it back with your hands. Cut off the tip of both ends. Cut the plantain in half lengthwise, and cut each half into 1-inch pieces.

Pour ½ inch oil into a large sauté pan and set over medium heat, until oil reaches 350°F.

Working in batches, fry the plantain pieces, turning once until they are deep golden brown across the surface and caramelized around the edges, 12 minutes. Remove the plantains from the oil and drain on a wire rack or a plate set with paper towels.

Toss the golden brown pieces of fried plantains with the onion, ginger powder, and chile or red pepper flakes while still warm. Season to taste with salt and serve immediately.

A classic northern street food, this small plate of fermented rice cakes is perfect as a snack or for soaking up your favorite stews and soups. As with most fermented foods, time is your friend. Each step in making masa is meant to cultivate just the right amount of sourness in the batter, so that the vessel for your sauces and stews brings its own unique flavor.

The fermented rice paste itself will keep refrigerated for up to a month so you can do this step ahead. If you don't have a masa pan to make these puffed cakes, and don't care to purchase yet another cooking utensil, make these as Sinasir (fermented rice skillet cakes—page 204). Serve masa by itself lightly dusted with yaji spice, alongside Beef Suya (page 141) or drizzled with a little honey for a sweet treat.

Masa or Waina
(Fermented Rice Cakes)

YIELD: 24 CAKES

1 teaspoon instant yeast	Neutral oil, for frying
2½ cups Fermented Rice Paste (page 41)	Ground Yaji Spice Blend (page 95) or honey, for serving
2 teaspoons fine sea salt	

In a small bowl, combine the yeast with ½ cup warm water, stir until the yeast is dissolved and set aside. Pour the fermented rice paste into a medium bowl and stir in the salt. Pour the yeast mixture into the batter and stir to combine.

Cover with a clean kitchen linen and allow to rise until doubled in size, about 1 hour (at this point you can also leave the batter to ferment and develop more flavor by letting it rise slowly in the refrigerator over a 12-hour period). It should be doubled in size and foamy.

Stir the batter till smooth, making sure to get any paste that's settled along the bottom of the bowl. The batter should coat your spoon or spatula and leave streaks on the surface when poured off the spatula.

Over medium-high heat, warm up a well-seasoned small masa pan. Brush the insides of the holes generously with oil. Pour in about 2 tablespoons of the batter per hole. Cook until the surface is bubbling and the batter is cooked around the edges. Using a spatula or toothpick to loosen the cake, flip each cake to cook the other side until golden brown, about 3 to 4 minutes. Transfer the masa to a bowl and sprinkle with yaji spice or drizzle with honey. Transfer to a plate. Repeat the cooking process with the remaining batter, adding more oil as necessary, until all the batter is cooked off.

My mother assigns certain Nigerian dishes to the people with whom she first shared them, because the memory of the experience and the dish are intrinsically linked. I carry this with me too. Often when I say I am making a dish my mother taught me to make, I recall a name from the distant past—perhaps someone I've never met—whom my mother first told me was the dish's true ambassador.

This dish has always been explained to me as something my grandmother loved, even though I never shared it with her. "Oma George, your grandmother, loved her òjòjò with green ata rodo and finely minced onions," my mother would say. As I wrote down her instructions for the dish, I thought of all the ways in which the women in my family have guided my hands while creating this book. Oma George passed on in 2010, but she remains at the center of my culinary memories and is among the most important influences in my understanding of Nigerian cuisine.

Òjòjò is a fritter made with a seasonal variety of yam called "water yam," which has a high moisture content and a certain draw or elasticity (similar to grated okra). I've made this version with the fresh yams that I find at Terminal Market in Brooklyn. The batter, made from grated yams, is true to how my grandmother liked it, but you should experiment with garlic, scallions, chopped red chiles, or other additions that will hold up well in the mixture.

#

**SERVES 6 TO 8
(YIELDS ABOUT
32 PIECES)**

2 pounds yams
(about 2 medium)

1 cup finely
chopped yellow
onion

1 green Scotch
bonnet pepper,
stemmed and
minced

½ teaspoon fine
sea salt

4 cups vegetable
or other neutral
oil such as
grapeseed,
sunflower, or
canola oil, for
frying

Ata Dín Dín
(page 93), for
serving (optional)

NOTE For consistently crisp results, use the large blades of a box grater and go with new yams versus old ones (see guide page 36). Add an egg or a tablespoon of cornstarch if you sense that the batter needs some help with binding. Fry quickly in hot neutral oil to a crisp, light tan color.

continued >

Ọ̀jọ̀jọ̀

< continued

Remove the skin on the roots by peeling with a paring knife or a vegetable peeler. Move the peeled roots to a bowl of water to keep them from turning brown.

Using the large side of a box grater, grate the peeled yams into a bowl. (Alternatively, you can do this with a food processor and pulse to a coarse puree.) Stir in the onion and Scotch bonnet pepper. Add the salt and fold the ingredients gently to combine.

Heat the oil to 350°F. Working in batches, use a spoon to transfer tablespoon-size portions to the hot oil. Fry until cooked through and a light golden brown, turning frequently to cook evenly on all sides, about 6 minutes. Remove from the oil and drain on a cooling rack inserted in a baking sheet or a plate lined with paper towels. Repeat the frying process, letting the oil return to temperature between batches, until the remaining batter is cooked. Serve while still warm, alone or with a side of ata dín dín for dipping.

Deep-fried milk curds?! With yaji spice?! I hope this combination thrills you as much as it does me. Great substitutes for wàrà in the diaspora are cheese curds, or fresh or frozen Indian paneer.

These little bites share a lot of the pleasures of fried food—with their crispy exterior and umami goodness—but they're suitable for anyone who doesn't eat meat. A great snack or appetizer, both fresh or fried wàrà can also be stirred into soups and stews as a meat replacement.

Wàrà WITH YAJI
(Deep-Fried Cheese Curds)

SERVES 4

- 8 ounces fresh Wàrà (page 48) or paneer, cut into 8 pieces
- Fine sea salt to taste
- Neutral oil, for frying
- 2 tablespoons Ground Yaji Spice Blend (page 95), for serving

Pat the wàrà pieces dry and season lightly with salt. Place a deep saucepan over medium-high heat and heat up 2 to 3 inches of oil to 350° to 375°F. Gently transfer the wàrà pieces to the oil and fry, turning frequently until golden brown on all sides, about 8 minutes.

Transfer to a plate lined with paper towels or to a baking rack to drain. Toss with yaji spice and enjoy while still warm.

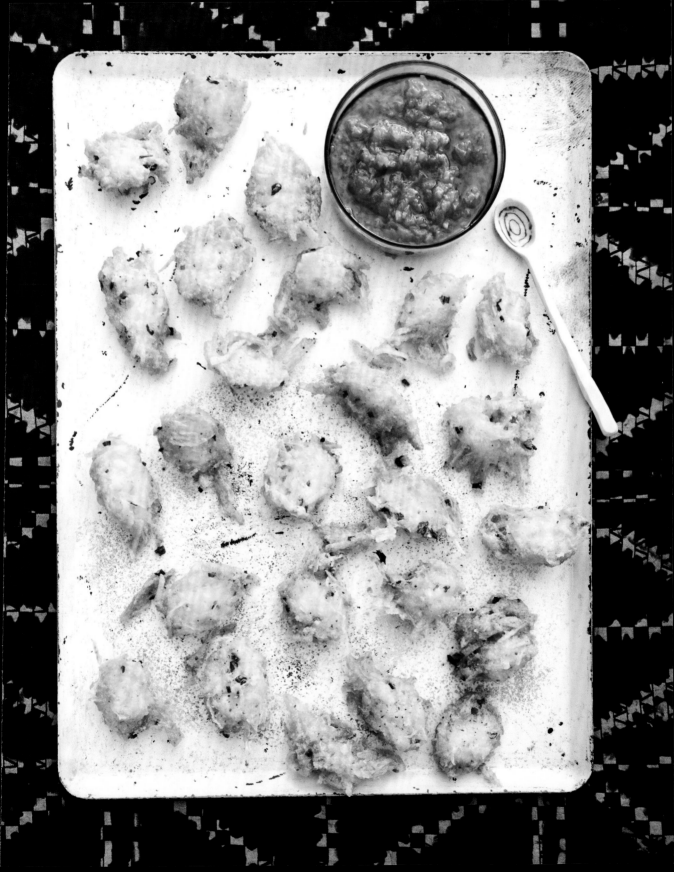

Hailing from the north, suya is a popular Nigerian street food made of thin strips of meat that are skewered, seasoned, and grilled. Different types of meat can be used to make suya, but it is typically made with beef. This recipe is similar in style to the suya made from a fattier cut of beef called "tozo," which comes from the hump of a Brahman cow. I recommend a well-marbled piece of boneless short rib. Get your butcher to thinly slice the meat into strips or pop the whole cut into your freezer for 30 minutes and use a sharp knife to slice.

Spice blends are available online or at African groceries. If you are feeling adventurous, the recipe on page 95 will get you close to the real thing. And don't skip the onion slices! While they are pretty as a garnish, they also add texture and freshness to the deep flavors of the grilled meat.

Beef Suya

YIELD: MAKES 4 SERVINGS (12 SKEWERS TOTAL)

1 pound boneless short ribs, thinly sliced lengthwise into ⅛-inch strips

¼ cup peanut oil, plus more for brushing and grilling

2 tablespoons Ground Yaji Spice Blend (page 95), plus more for garnish

1 (2-inch) piece fresh ginger, peeled and grated

2 garlic cloves, grated

1 tablespoon fine salt, plus more to taste

1 small red onion, peeled and thinly sliced into rings

Lay several strips of meat side by side and flat on a piece of plastic and top witn another piece of plastic. Pound the meat strips to flatten into a ⅛-inch-thick even layer. Set aside and repeat with remaining meat.

In a medium bowl, combine the ¼ cup peanut oil and 2 tablespoons yaji spice blend with the ginger and garlic. Add the beef, toss to coat, and season with 1 tablespoon salt. Cover with plastic wrap and allow the beef to marinate refrigerated for at least 4 hours and as many as 12 hours.

Preheat a cleaned gas grill or grill plate to medium-high. Wipe the grill slates clean and brush with an oiled towel to create a nonstick layer.

Skewer the beef pieces in an even layer on individual wooden skewers, wiping off any excess marinade. Brush the meat generously with more oil and set the skewers on a baking sheet.

Working in batches, grill the beef skewers until meat is cooked through and lightly charred on both sides, 6 to 7 minutes per side. Transfer the skewers to a platter and sprinkle with more yaji spice blend. Repeat until all the beef has been grilled.

Serve the suya warm, topped with the raw onions and alongside additional yaji spice for dipping.

NOTE To thinly slice beef, freeze the short ribs until just beginning to firm up around the edges, about 30 minutes. Slice using a sharp knife.

Driving in Lagos requires both vigilance and creativity. Often, you'll end up circling the same routes countless times in fruitless attempts to outwit traffic. On my last visit, I would pass the same vendor on Agidingbi Road day after day, marveling at the neatly stacked foil packs placed in front of his stall.

Inside were his peppered chicken gizzards, the perfect small chop for meat lovers: bite-size portions of cooked meats and sautéed peppers, tossed in a fiery sauce. Like suya, it's one of the few small chops that centers meat as the main attraction.

I have served peppered chicken gizzards as a tasting course at my dinners because they presage the flavors and heat that will be evoked by subsequent courses. Fried snails and bite-sized chunks of cooked chicken, beef, lamb, or goat are all options here. Lightly sautéed bell peppers are traditional, but I've opted for the crisp acidic bite of quick-pickled baby peppers, a garnish that can be done days ahead.

Peppered Chicken Gizzards

SERVES 4 TO 6

QUICK-PICKLED BABY BELL PEPPERS

¼ cup freshly squeezed lime juice (from about 5 limes)

½ teaspoon salt

8 baby bell peppers, stemmed and thinly sliced, or 1 medium bell pepper (any color would do)

GIZZARDS

2 tablespoons grapeseed oil

1 pound cooked chicken gizzards, lamb, beef, or goat chunks in 1-inch pieces

1 small onion, thinly sliced

1 cup Ata Dín Dín (page 93)

Fine salt to taste

For the Quick-Pickled Baby Bell Peppers
In a small bowl, combine the lime juice with ½ teaspoon salt and stir to dissolve the salt. Add the sliced peppers and set aside.

For the Gizzards
Heat the oil in a shallow pan over medium heat. Add the chicken gizzards and sauté, stirring frequently until golden brown on all sides, about 12 minutes. Add the onion and sauté until just beginning to soften, 4 minutes. Add the ata dín dín and stir to coat the gizzard pieces in the sauce. Allow to simmer until the sauce is warmed through, adjusting the seasoning with salt if necessary. Serve the gizzards warm, garnished with several slices of pickled pepper and additional ata dín dín for dipping.

NOTE Gizdòdò is a variation where the peppered gizzards are tossed with dòdò and ata dín dín.

Not to be confused with the American sweet potato, the West African yam is a large, starchy, and dense root vegetable common in the "Yam Belt" of Benin, Cameroon, Côte d'Ivoire, Ghana, Nigeria, and Togo. After its skin is peeled with a sharp knife or vegetable peeler, its stark bright white, cream, or soft yellow flesh is ready for boiling, roasting or, in the case of dun dun, frying.

Dun dun is the Yorùbá name for the crispy yam fries that are a popular snack and side dish across Lagos. They can be shallow-fried in oil or roasted over coals for a drier version. Serve fries warm with some Ata Dín Dín (page 93), your favorite condiment, or just a sprinkling of salt.

Fried Chips
(Yam, Cassava, Potato, or Plantain)

SERVES 4

FOR STARCHY ROOTS (YAM, CASSAVA, COCOYAM, OR SWEET POTATO)

Fine salt

1 pound root vegetable (about 1 medium tuber)

4 cups vegetable oil or other neutral oil such as grapeseed, sunflower, or canola, for frying

Ata Dín Dín (page 93), for serving

FOR PLANTAINS

1 pound green plantains

4 cups vegetable or other neutral oil such as grapeseed, sunflower, or canola oil, for frying

Fine salt to taste

Ata Dín Dín (page 93), for serving

For Starchy Roots

Bring a large pot of water to a boil over medium heat and season generously with salt.

Fill a large bowl with water. Slice off the ends of the tuber and cut into 1-inch-thick disks. Use a peeler or sharp knife to peel off the brown skin. Drop peeled pieces into the bowl of water as you peel to prevent the tuber from oxidizing and browning. Once sliced and peeled, cut each disk into ½-inch-wide matchsticks. You should get five or six sticks per disk.

Working in batches, drop the cut matchsticks into the simmering water and blanch for 2 to 3 minutes. Remove

from the hot water and drain on a rack inserted in a baking sheet. Repeat the blanching and draining process for the remaining tuber pieces.

Fill a large skillet with oil about 1½ inches from the bottom (if you're using a 9-inch skillet, you'll need about 4 cups of oil) and heat to 350°F using an instant-read thermometer. Working in batches to avoid overcrowding, fry the matchsticks until golden brown and crispy, 10 to 12 minutes. Remove from the oil and drain on a baking sheet lined with paper towels or a wire rack. Season the fries with salt. Repeat this step until all the yam has been fried. (I did this in two batches.)

Serve fries warm with some ata dín dín or your favorite condiment on the side.

For Plantains

Peel the plantains by using a sharp knife to make a slit in the skin (avoid cutting the flesh) down the middle, and remove the skin by peeling it back with your hands. Cut off the tip of both ends. Using a sharp knife or a mandoline, carefully slice the plantain or potatoes into thin (about ⅛-inch-thick) slices.

Fill a large skillet with oil up to about 1½ inches (4 cups in a 9-inch skillet) from the bottom and heat to 350°F using an instant read thermometer. Working in batches to avoid overcrowding, fry the plantain until golden brown and crispy, 10 to 12 minutes. Remove from the oil and drain on a baking sheet lined with paper towels or a wire rack. Season with salt. Repeat this step until all the plantain slices have been fried.

Serve warm or at room temperature, alone or with ata dín dín for dipping.

NOTE Yams can be easily found at any West African, Caribbean, or Hispanic market. They are large tubers with a rough brown exterior and a crisp, white interior. They sometimes come in a variety that is pale yellow on the inside; these are less starchy but similar in taste. Grocers will typically have a cut tuber available to show the variety and how fresh the tubers are.

Yams have a long shelf life but will show signs of decay if they haven't been stored properly. Check the yams for freshness by pressing down on the skin along the tuber. It should withstand the pressure of your fingers. Softness, indentations, or dried spots that go through the tuber are all signs the yam has gone bad.

I wrote a version of this recipe with a dusting of spiced sugar for my *New York Times* article "Ten Essential Nigerian Recipes," in 2019. This version below is what I refer to as my template recipe. Puff puff is so versatile that it lends itself to many adaptations. Typically served plain without spiced sugar, puff puff can also be found sweet or savory or stuffed. They are an irresistible snack, and any leftovers will store well frozen or refrigerated, ready to be popped in the oven when needed. These are best enjoyed while warm.

Puff Puff

YIELD: 8 TO 10 SERVINGS (ABOUT 32 PUFFS)

1½ cups (360 milliliters) warm water or whole milk (110°F)

4 teaspoons (15 grams) active dry yeast

⅔ cup (135 grams) granulated sugar

3 cups (385 grams) all-purpose flour

1 tablespoon (10 grams) kosher salt

½ teaspoon grated nutmeg

4 cups vegetable or other neutral oil such as grapeseed, sunflower, or canola oil, for frying

In a small bowl, whisk together the warm water, yeast, and 1 tablespoon sugar. Let sit until foamy, 8 to 10 minutes.

In a separate bowl, combine the flour, salt, nutmeg, and the remaining sugar. Make a well in the center and pour in the yeast mixture once it's foamy. Combine, stirring with a wooden spoon, to incorporate all the ingredients into a smooth batter. The batter should be wet and slightly loose, similar to a yeasted waffle batter.

Cover the bowl with a clean kitchen towel and allow the batter to double in size, about 40 minutes.

Pour 1 inch of oil into a large, deep skillet. Line a baking sheet with a rack or paper towels to absorb excess oil.

Once the batter has doubled in size, heat the oil over medium high to 350°F. Drop tablespoonfuls of batter into the hot oil, working in batches to avoid crowding the skillet. Fry the puff puffs, turning frequently until golden brown all over and cooked through, 5 to 6 minutes per batch. (Be careful not to let the oil get too hot or the exteriors will become overly dark before the interiors are cooked through.)

Move the puff puffs to the rack or paper towels to drain and repeat the process until all the batter has been fried.

Enjoy warm or at room temperature.

DAYTIME: WEEKDAY MEALS AND THE BUKA MENU

Buka is a concept, a space we relate to food when we are out in the streets of Lagos. The buka is typically a small eatery, but sometimes it's just a counter in a wall. Tables are turned quickly and the masses can be nourished. Gossip and business matters intermingle at the buka. Buka food is the way we describe anything from a short to lengthy lunch. It's the closest thing to a home-cooked meal that can be had while out and about.

These are the dishes you will encounter in restaurants and cafés, cafeterias and bars, roadside stands and government complexes, nightclubs and church dining halls, airports and home kitchens. Some restaurants in Lagos have their noontime lunch rush, but others will see a steady stream of diners setting up midday. Daytime cuisine in Lagos can be packaged to take away or served multi-course in a setting where business and pleasure intermingle.

Clearly defined categories of breakfast, lunch, and

dinner foods do not exist in Lagos. Foods typically consumed in the morning, as well as most small chops, will often accompany meals served late into the day. Collected here are the recipes that provide the anchors of a great midday, afternoon, or dinner menu. These dishes are meant to be convivial and communal.

Their portion sizes are dictated not by the recipes themselves but by the hunger of the person making them. Some are one-pot meals that can serve three or four, or even be stretched out to eight people or more. Others are stews that can be eaten on their own or as accompaniments. No one dish is a focal point, but all of them could be. Some must be served immediately, piping hot; others are brilliant for storing, freezing, and reheating when needed.

There is a harmony to eating this way. Although the focus is to provide flavor and satiate hunger, these dishes are nutrient rich and deeply fulfilling. They are called "daytime" meals, but their attachment to a particular time of day is more a coincidence than a rule.

ALÀSÉPÒ, POTTAGE, ONE-POT MEALS

These are meals built for convenience. Made in a single pot, these dishes start out as flavorful saucy bases to which starchy vegetables are typically added. The vegetables thicken the sauce while absorbing the flavors in the pot. Alàsépò meals are endlessly adaptable and can be made with or without animal protein. For the time-challenged cook, they can be quick weeknight meal options. Time is the friend of the cook who loves to plan ahead, as flavors, aroma and even textures improve when the ingredients are given the chance to mingle in the pot. I love to finish these by stirring in a handful of leafy greens, and with a shower of fresh herbs.

Okra, a rich source of fiber, magnesium, and vitamins, is the star of this dish. In Yorùbá, àsepò means "to cook together," and ilá àsepò is my ultimate everything-in-one-pot soup. The ingredients can vary according to preference or what you have available: fresh fish, shrimp, meat, tripe, or whatever else you believe goes well with okra's slippery texture. For me, àsepò is comfort food, a wonderful combination of fragrant and familiar ingredients.

Ilá àsepò can serve as a midweek quick fix when you want to stretch some leftover stew. I use fresh ata lílò here, but use any leftover ọbẹ ata as a base to build on the other ingredients; the okra will do the rest. When it comes to draw soups, the "àsepò method" is primarily used for Ilá and Ogbono (page 166); here, it is finished with a spoonful or two of red palm oil.

Ilá Àsepò

SERVES 4

2 tablespoons grapeseed oil

1 small yellow onion, chopped

2 tablespoons Trinity Pepper Paste (page 102) or 1 red Scotch bonnet pepper, whole

2 cups Ata Lílò (page 90)

3 cups meat stock (page 79), vegetable stock, or water

3 loose cups fresh okra (8 to 10 ounces)

1 pound cooked assorted meat or roast mushrooms (see page 166)

½ cup (50 grams) stockfish, softened and torn into 1-inch pieces (page 75), or smoked fish pieces (see page 75)

2 tablespoon red palm oil

Fine salt to taste

1 tablespoon rehydrated bitter leaves or ¼ cup washed fresh leaves (optional)

Òkèlè (page 52), for serving

In a large pot, heat the grapeseed oil over medium-high heat. Add the onion and sauté until softened and translucent, about 5 minutes. Add the pepper paste and sauté until just fragrant, about 1 minute. Stir in the ata lílò and stock. Bring to a boil, lower the heat to medium, and allow the sauce to simmer until the flavors meld, the sauce thickens slightly, and oil begins to rise to the surface, about 15 minutes.

While the stew is simmering, use a box grater to coarsely grate the okra, holding each by the stem end to avoid brushing your knuckles. You can also coarsely chop the okra using a sharp knife.

Add the cooked meat or mushrooms, stock fish pieces, and red palm oil to the stew. Season with salt and simmer until the meat is warmed through, 10 to 12 minutes. If using fresh seafood pieces such as fish steaks or prawns, cook until the seafood is just tender and still slightly undercooked. The seafood will continue to cook once the okra is added in.

Add the grated okra and bitter leaves, if using, to the pot and stir gently to incorporate. Cook over medium-low heat and bring to a gentle simmer. Allow to simmer and cook just enough to warm the okra pieces, 4 to 5 minutes. Adjust the soup texture with additional water if you prefer a brothy soup. Remove from heat and season with additional salt to taste.

Ladle into shallow bowls and top with a helping of any Òkèlè (page 52), such as ẹ̀bà, àmàlà, or pounded yam.

Àsáró in Yorùbá refers to a pottage dish anchored by a starchy vegetable cooked in a flavorful broth. The vegetable pieces soften in the broth, thickening the liquid as they cook. Àsáró can be made with any combination of root vegetables, such as yams and potatoes, or plantains, or even corn. The yam will cook down eventually, but that's its charm: it builds texture within the finished soup. A few cups of any leafy greens will be a welcome addition. The greens you pick should add a little bitterness or citrus flavor, depending on the variety. In Lagos, àsáró is typically topped with stewed meats as a hearty lunch or early dinner.

Àsáró

SERVES 6 TO 8

¼ cup neutral oil such as canola or grapeseed

1 small red or yellow onion, thinly sliced

4 garlic cloves, smashed

2 tablespoons minced fresh ginger

2 tablespoons Trinity Pepper Paste (page 102) or 1 teaspoon red pepper flakes (optional)

2 tablespoons tomato paste

One 14.5-ounce can whole peeled tomatoes

Fine salt to taste

2½ pounds white or yellow yams (or any other starchy root vegetable, or green plantains), peeled and cut into 1½-inch pieces

¼ cup red palm oil

4 cups chopped mustard greens, or other leafy greens such as spinach, turnip, beet (optional)

¼ cup cilantro leaves and tender stems

¼ cup julienned efirin or tulsi basil leaves

Meat in Ọbẹ̀ Dín Dín (see headnote, page 193), for serving

In a large pot or Dutch oven, heat the neutral oil over medium until shimmering, 1 to 2 minutes. Add the onion, garlic, ginger, and pepper paste, if using, to the pot and sauté until fragrant, about 2 minutes. Add the tomato paste and cook until darkened to a brick red, about 2 minutes. Add the whole peeled tomatoes plus any liquid, crushing the tomatoes with your hands as they go in. Stir and scrape the bottom of the pot to combine the ingredients and disperse the tomato paste.

Pour in 3 cups water and bring to a boil over high heat. Once boiling, season with salt, reduce the heat to medium, and allow to simmer. Add the yam pieces. Cook until just tender, about 15 minutes. Using a wooden spoon or fork, crush the yam pieces into the body of the liquid. You should end up with a chunky, thickened stew. Stir in the red palm oil and chopped greens

if using, season with more salt, and simmer for another 10 minutes.

Remove from heat and serve hot, garnished with fresh cilantro and efirin, alongside the stewed meat.

NOTE Cassava, cocoyam (taro root), sweet potatoes, and plantains can substitute for the yam in this recipe. You can also add a mix of starches, such as the combinations of yam and plantains, sweet potatoes and cocoyam, plantains and corn, and so on. Keep the ratios about the same (total of 2½ pounds) and you'll end up with similar results.

Preparing this rice and chicken one-pot meal is an experience: the rich fragrances of these ingredients will slowly fill your kitchen as the rice softens. Iwuk edesi is a dish rooted in Efik and Ibibio cuisine, a gift from the southeastern region of the country. It is often found on buka menus and is sometimes called "native rice." If you use another type of meat, the cooking times may differ, but the method essentially stays the same. This is a solid stand-alone meal, best enjoyed straight off the stove, but is equally satisfying the next day as leftovers.

Iwuk Edesi WITH CHICKEN
(One-Pot Native Rice with Chicken)

SERVES 6 TO 8

¼ cup neutral oil such as canola or grapeseed

3 pounds bone-in, skin-on chicken parts

Fine salt to taste

1 tablespoon grated ginger

2 garlic cloves, smashed

½ cup red palm oil

2 tablespoons Trinity Pepper Paste (page 102)

2 cups long grain white rice

About 2¼ cups chicken stock (page 79)

4 cups torn hearty greens such as ugwu, mature spinach, collards, or kale

1 small red onion, finely chopped

In a large pot or Dutch oven, heat the oil over medium until shimmering, 1 to 2 minutes.

Pat the chicken pieces dry and season both sides generously with salt. Working in batches if necessary, place the chicken pieces skin side down in the pot and sear until deep golden brown on both sides, about 12 minutes total. Move the seared pieces to a plate and set aside.

Drain out all but 2 tablespoons oil. Add the ginger and garlic and stir until fragrant. Stir in the palm oil and pepper paste and then the rice. Stir to coat every grain of rice in the sea-soned oil. Add the stock. Scrape the bottom of the pot to loosen up any stuck bits, season with salt, and bring to a simmer. Do not stir the rice at this point.

Transfer the chicken to the pot skin side up, along with any liquid from the plate. Cover with the pot's lid or foil and cook until the liquid is absorbed, the rice is tender, and the chicken is cooked through, about 20 minutes. Stir in the greens and allow to wilt and soften, 2 minutes.

Remove from the heat and let sit covered for an additional 10 minutes. Carefully fluff the rice with a fork. Divide the rice and chicken among plates, sprinkle on the chopped red onion, and serve warm.

Ubek is a savory dish in which fresh corn soaks up the juicy flavors building in your pot. Though frozen corn will work, fresh sweet corn is best. This corn stew comes together much like our other one-pot stews àsáró and èwà rírò, and highlights the very best of what fresh seasonal corn has to offer. This version contains smoked fish and meat stock—but you can omit these to make this dish vegetarian. It is from the southeast of Nigeria and is traditionally served as a pottage on its own.

Smoked catfish and hot peppers, lightened with fresh herbs, all build to a heady, sumptuous delicacy.

Ubek (Corn Stew with Smoked Catfish)

SERVES 4 TO 6

- 2 tablespoons neutral oil such as vegetable or grapeseed oil
- 1 small red onion, minced
- 1 tablespoon Trinity Pepper Paste (page 102)
- 6 cups fresh corn kernels (from about 8 ears)
- 2 cups meat or chicken stock (page 79) or vegetable stock
- Fine salt to taste
- 2 tablespoons red palm oil

- 1 cup flaked smoked catfish, skin and bones discarded (page 75)
- 4 cups thinly sliced greens such as ugwu, mature spinach, collards or kale
- ¼ cup scent leaf or thai basil leaves, thinly sliced
- ¼ cup fresh cilantro leaves, chopped
- ¼ cup fresh mint leaves
- 1 lime, cut into wedges for squeezing

Heat the oil in a large sauté pan set over medium heat. Add the minced onions and sauté until just beginning to soften, 2 to 3 minutes. Add the trinity pepper paste and stir until fragrant. Stir in the corn and stock and bring to a simmer. Allow to cook until the corn is tender and the stock is reduced by half its original volume, about 8 minutes. Season with salt, add the red palm oil, and stir in the smoked catfish and greens. Cook until the greens are wilted and tender and the fish is warmed through, 3 to 4 minutes.

In a small bowl, toss together the scent leaf or basil, cilantro, and mint. Spoon the porridge into wide shallow bowls and garnish with a handful of the herb mix and lime slices for squeezing.

This is my father's specialty, a fresh and brothy fish stew with hearty dumplings reserved for Friday evenings. He'd put on *Fela Ransome Kuti and His Koola Lobitos* and a large array of highlife classics and get to work, cleaning the whole fish he'd grabbed from the market on his way home, stirring the pot of his spicy àlapa bubbling away behind him, and salting the just-grated yam waiting in a bowl.

The trick to this recipe is to stop stirring the sauce the moment the fish goes in. This soup is perfect for humid afternoons, rainy days, or whenever you need a light broth to satiate a strong hunger.

Dad's Àlapa
WITH FRESH CATFISH AND DUMPLINGS

SERVES 4 TO 6

STEW

2 tablespoons red palm oil

1 small red onion, chopped

4 garlic cloves, sliced

2 tablespoons tomato paste

4 cups Ata Lílò (page 90)

3 cups vegetable, fish (page 80), or chicken stock (page 79)

1 pound catfish, grouper, or snapper fillets, cut into 1-inch cubes

DUMPLINGS

1 pound yam, peeled and immersed in cold water to keep from browning

¼ cup minced red onion

¼ cup sliced green onion or scallions, trimmed and sliced

½ teaspoon fine salt

½ teaspoon freshly cracked atare seeds

TO SERVE

¼ cup chopped dill or tarragon leaves

¼ cup julienned scent leaf

1 lemon, zest reserved, sliced into wedges for squeezing

In a large pot, heat the oil over medium-high heat. Add the onion and sauté until softened and translucent, about 5 minutes. Add the garlic and sauté until just fragrant, about 1 minute. Add the tomato paste and cook until darkened to a deep red, 2 to 3 minutes more. Stir in the ata lílò and stock. Bring to a boil and allow to simmer until slightly reduced, 12 to 15 minutes.

While the stew is simmering, use the fine side of a box grater to grate all the peeled yam pieces into a medium bowl. (You can also do this with a food processor: Roughly chop the yam and pulse to a coarse puree, then transfer to a bowl.) Stir in the minced onion and green onion, then add the salt and atare. Fold the ingredients gently to combine into a soft dough.

Lower the heat on the stew and drop teaspoonfuls of dumpling dough into the liquid until all the dough has been used. The dumplings will thicken the stew as they cook. Let the stew gently simmer until the dumplings float to the surface, 18 to 20 minutes. Gently add the catfish pieces and allow the seafood to cook until the fish flakes easily and the flesh is firm, 4 to 5 minutes.

continued >

Dad's Àlapa

< continued

Combine the dill, scent leaf, and zest of the lemon in a small bowl. Divide the stew, dumplings, and fish pieces among 4 to 6 bowls and top with the herb mixture and a squeeze of lemon.

NOTE Àlapa is used here in reference to a brothy version of the basic ata sauce. This is what my family called these brothy soups in which fresh seafood was the star. I can't confirm that this is an accurate description of àlapa, as it also shows up in reference to a palm oil stew or a steamed dumpling dish made with ègúsí.

Thickened Soups, Stewed Meats, and Seafood

Each of the soups in this section contain an ingredient that specifically add viscosity, thickness or creaminess. Thickeners can range from nuts and seeds to leafy greens and ground spices. Each soup is named for the ingredient that thickens it. For example, ègúsí soup is thickened with ègúsí seeds, ilá soup is thickened by the okra and so on. When we refer to draw soups, we mean that the soup has viscosity and body.

Common ingredients that can thicken soups include:

Nuts and seeds: groundnuts, ègúsí, benne seed, dried okra seeds, dried ogbono seeds, achi seeds, okobo seeds

Dried and fresh vegetables: fresh okra, milkweed, kuka, moringa

Fats: palm fruit, manshanu

Starches: cooked and pounded starches can also be used as a thickening agent; see Oha Soup (page 185) and Ofe Nsala (page 236)

Ilá is a soup made from seasoned, grated fresh okra that you eat topped with a stew. Ilá is also the Yorùbá name for the ingredient, okra. Because this is a soup with very few ingredients, each must hold its own. Your okra must be fresh, your irú plump and fragrant. You can vary the thickness of the soup with the addition of more liquid, but I prefer a thicker consistency.

Eaten with swallows (see page 52), it's a simple soup that's meant to be an accompaniment.

Ilá (Grated Okra)

YIELD: 4 CUPS

1 pound fresh okra

½ teaspoon fine salt, plus more to taste

1 tablespoon dried crayfish, soaked in hot water

1 tablespoon irú (fermented locust bean), soaked in hot water

Ọbẹ̀ Dín Dín (see headnote, page 93), for serving

Swallow/Òkèlè (page 52), for serving

Using a box grater, coarsely grate the okra holding each by the stem end to avoid brushing your knuckles. Place the grated okra in a pot and add 1½ to 2 cups water, depending on how thick you want the soup, and the salt.

Drain the crayfish and irú and add to the pot. Cook over medium-low heat and bring up to a gentle simmer. Allow to simmer for 4 to 5 minutes, just enough to warm up and cook the okra pieces until it turns bright green and the soup begins to bubble. Remove from the heat, season with salt to taste. Serve topped with a generous spoon of meat in ọbẹ̀ dín dín, alongside a swallow.

Sometimes reconnecting with an ingredient from my past is often all I need for my memories to find expression in the form of a recipe. When my friend Yemi brought over a bag of fresh jute leaves that she had picked from her farm, I was transported to the garden of my parents' old home in Ikeja—a garden I last saw as a teenager headed to university in the United States. Those leaves were plentiful in that old garden.

When I saw Yemi's fresh jute leaves, I immediately knew how I was going to use them. I pulsed them in my food processor with a little liquid. Touched with a little salt and heated gently in a pot, the resulting soup had the perfect draw. This is the reward, I felt, for carrying these food stories with me. Once given the ingredients, I could finally bring my memories to life.

Jute leaves are hallmarks in a number of global regional dishes such as the Togolese adémè déssi, Egyptian molokhia, and Haitian lalo to name a few. The leaves are delightful in their flavor, texture, and nutritional content.

Ewédú

SERVES 4

1 packed cup frozen jute leaves, squeezed dry, or 4 loose cups fresh jute leaves

½ teaspoon fine salt, plus more to taste

1 tablespoon dried crayfish, soaked in hot water

1 teaspoon irú (fermented locust bean), soaked in hot water

Ọbẹ̀ Dín Dín (see headnote, page 93), for serving

Swallow (page 52), for serving

In a blender or a food processor, combine the jute leaves with 1 cup water and puree until smooth. Pour the puree into a small saucepan, and add the salt, drained crayfish, and irú. Bring to a gentle simmer over low heat, stirring occasionally to combine, and allow the soup to heat through, about 3 minutes.

Remove from the heat and serve topped with a generous helping of meat in a pool of ọbẹ̀ dín dín, alongside a swallow.

This is a market favorite of mine—a ready-to-eat grilled fish with a fresh, peppery sauce. Fish with a high oil content, such as mackerel, tilapia, croaker, or trout is most often used, but any tender white fish will work well. Serve this hot, and top it with spoonfuls of fresh ata lílọ̀, pepper paste, or ata dín dín, alongside steamed rice or cold Soaked Garri (page 49). It's fresh, light, and profoundly invigorating.

Whole Roast Fish
WITH ATA LÍLỌ̀

SERVES 4

4 whole fish scaled and cleaned (about 3½ pounds mackerel, tilapia, croaker, trout, or branzino)

½ cup neutral oil such as grapeseed oil, safflower, or canola

Fine salt

1 cup Ata Lílọ̀ (page 90), Trinity Pepper Paste (page 102), or Ata Dín Dín (page 93), plus more for serving

1 teaspoon ground atare seeds

½ cup fresh cilantro leaves and tender stems

¼ cup sliced green onions

Lime, sliced into wedges for squeezing

Cooked rice or roasted vegetables (page 61), such as plantains, yams, or cassava, for serving

Heat the oven to 450°F. Pat the body and inside of the fish dry, and space the fish evenly apart on an unlined sheet pan. Using a sharp knife, cut two diagonal slits, 2 inches apart, into the skin of each fish, making sure not to cut through to the bone. Repeat the slits on the other side. Drizzle both sides and the inside of each fish with 1 tablespoon oil, and season each with 1 teaspoon salt.

Roast the fish until firm and cooked through, rotating the sheet pan once halfway through the process, about 22 to 25 minutes.

While the fish is roasting, season the ata lílọ̀ and pour it into a small bowl. Stir in the remaining oil and ground atare and set aside.

Turn the oven to broil and allow the fish to cook until the skin is browned and charred in spots, 5 to 6 minutes. Remove from the oven.

Transfer the roasted fish to individual plates. Dress each with a spoonful of ata lílọ̀, a sprinkling of the cilantro and green onions, and a squeeze of lime. Serve with steamed rice or roasted vegetables, and more ata lílọ̀.

My husband describes ogbono soup as having an elastic consistency that quickly fills the space where your spoon has just been. The first time he ordered it, at the lovely Houston restaurant Cafe Abuja, he couldn't believe how viscous it was when pushed with his spoon. "This is a soup that draws," I told him before he ordered it, referring to the expansive stretch in the liquid. He later confessed to me, "I had no idea what you were talking about."

Ogbono

SERVES 4 TO 6

1 cup dried ogbono seeds

3 cups meat stock (page 79), vegetable stock, or water

2 tablespoons grapeseed oil

1 small yellow onion, chopped

2 tablespoons Trinity Pepper Paste (page 102) or 1 red Scotch bonnet pepper, whole

2 cups Ata Lílò (page 90)

1 pound cooked assorted meat or roast mushrooms (recipe follows)

½ cup (50 grams) stockfish, softened and torn into 1-inch pieces (page 75, optional)

2 tablespoon red palm oil

Fine salt to taste

1 tablespoon rehydrated bitter leaves (optional)

Òkèlè (page 52), for serving

ROAST MUSHROOMS

2 pounds mixed mushrooms such as button, oyster, cremini, and shiitake, cleaned, trimmed and torn or cut into 2-inch pieces

6 to 8 thyme sprigs

½ cup neutral oil such as grapeseed

Fine sea salt

For the Ogbono
Using a spice mill or food processor, pulse the ogbono seeds into a finely ground powder. Work in batches if necessary. In a small bowl, combine the ground ogbono with 1 cup of the stock or water.

In a large pot, heat the grapeseed oil over medium-high heat. Add onion and sauté until softened, about 3 minutes. Add the trinity pepper paste or Scotch bonnet pepper and sauté until just fragrant, 1 minute. Stir in the ata lílò and the rest of the stock or water. Bring to a boil, lower the heat to medium. Allow sauce to simmer until it thickens slightly, and oil begins to rise to the surface, about 15 minutes.

Add the cooked meat or roast mushrooms, stockfish pieces, and red palm oil. Season the stew with salt and simmer until the meat is warmed through, 10 to 12 minutes.

Stir in the ogbono paste and use a whisk to gently break it up into the body of the soup. The soup will begin to thicken and foam around the edges. Lower the heat and simmer the soup until thick and large bubbles rise to the surface, 4 to 6 minutes. Add the bitter leaves, if using, and cook for 1 to 2 minutes.

Adjust the soup texture with additional water if you prefer a brothy soup. Remove from the heat and season with additional salt to taste. Ladle into shallow bowls and serve with a helping of any Òkèlè (page 52).

For the Roast Mushrooms
Heat the oven to 425°F. Spread the mushrooms and thyme sprigs in an even layer on a sheet pan and drizzle the oil on top. Season with salt and, using your hands, toss to coat. Roast, turning the pan halfway through and tossing the mushrooms, until they are golden brown and crisp along the edges, 25 to 35 minutes.

You'll find this classic dish of a whole fish bubbling away in a vat of hot oil on menus in Lagos and across the diaspora. We all need a good buka, and this recipe seeks to approximate the experience of seeing this arrive at a table fresh out of the kitchen. Still, if you can clear some space to set up a frying station, this home-fried fish will not disappoint. Seasoned liberally and fried until crisp, the result is textural and aromatic bliss.

Make sure to pat the fish dry completely before frying. Serve hot with ata dín dín sauce for dipping. Condiments like yaji spice (page 95), pepper paste (page 102), or tamarind paste (page 98) also shine here.

Now, if you know what's good, you know that the fried fish's head is a thing of beauty because it yields the crispiest little bites. And I know you know what's good.

Crispy Fried Tilapia

SERVES 4

2½ to 3 pounds whole tilapia, cleaned and gutted with head on

About 4 cups neutral oil (such as grapeseed, canola or safflower), for frying

1 tablespoon ground atare or Ground Yaji Spice Blend (page 95)

2 teaspoons fine salt

1 red onion, peeled and thinly sliced

Ata Dín Dín (page 93), heated, for serving

Pat the fish dry using a clean towel or paper towels. Set a baking rack inside a rimmed baking sheet or line a large plate with paper towels. Heat the oil in a wide, shallow skillet over medium-high heat. In a small bowl, combine the ground atare or yaji spice and fine sea salt. Rub the salt mixture into the skin and on the inside of the fish.

Working in batches, transfer the fish, head first, into the oil, carefully dropping the body in without splashing hot oil. Fry until the fish, turning once until it is cooked through, golden brown, and crispy, about 5 to 6 minutes per side. Transfer the fried fish to the cooling rack or plate to drain. Repeat the frying process for the remaining fish.

Serve hot garnished generously with raw onion and ata dín dín on the side for dipping.

Banga soup is a rich stew that draws its flavors from palm fruit, leafy greens, and a variety of fresh and dried fish. The process begins with fresh palm fruits steamed in water to loosen their pulpy flesh. The fruits are pounded, the hard kernels strained out, and the fibrous pulp is pressed to release a floral-tasting, creamy liquid. This becomes the soup's elegant base. In Brooklyn, I buy a canned version of this palm fruit base. It's a convenient option, and one that epitomizes the experience that West African immigrants like me know well: we relive our food memories through our resourcefulness, recreating our food system as best we can wherever we are.

Fresh catfish is best for this soup, but any other seafood or roasted mushroom mix will also work.

Banga Soup WITH CATFISH

YIELD: 2 CUPS

1 cup palm fruit concentrate

1 tablespoon Trinity Pepper Paste (page 102)

2 teaspoons ground store bought banga spice mix

1 oburunbebe stick or ½ teaspoon ground anise

½ cup (50 grams), stockfish, softened and torn into 1-inch pieces (page 75)

1 tablespoon dried beletete leaves or bitter leaf, rinsed (optional)

Fine salt to taste

1 medium whole catfish, cleaned and cut cross-wise into 2-inch pieces

½ cup fresh scent leaves or sweet leafy basil, thinly sliced

Èbà (see headnote, page 49), for serving

In a medium pot set over medium-high heat, add the palm fruit concentrate and 2 cups of water. Stir until well combined and bring to a boil. Reduce to a simmer, cooking the sauce until it reduces and thickens slightly; sections of red oil should begin to collect on the surface of the liquid, about 20 minutes.

Stir the pepper paste, banga spice, and oburunbebe stick or ground anise into the palm fruit sauce. Add the stockfish to the soup and the beletete leaves, if using. Cook until the sauce thickens and runs slowly off the back of a spoon, 8 to 10 minutes. Season with salt to taste.

Add the whole catfish and cook until it is cooked through and flakes if gently poked with a fork, 2 to 3 minutes for fillets and more time for 2-inch cross-sectioned chunks.

Garnish with scent leaves and serve immediately with èbà.

NOTE Naturally, banga soup is popular in areas where oil palm trees grow. Delta-style banga soup, popular in the south and southeast, is often made with a spice blend and a variety of herbs, including beletete leaf or bitterleaf, and is typically served in a clay pot with a swallow as accompaniment. Leafy greens or scent leaf can be added to other versions, and it also pairs well with rice. To make it vegetarian, skip the catfish and stockfish pieces and stir in sautéed mushrooms.

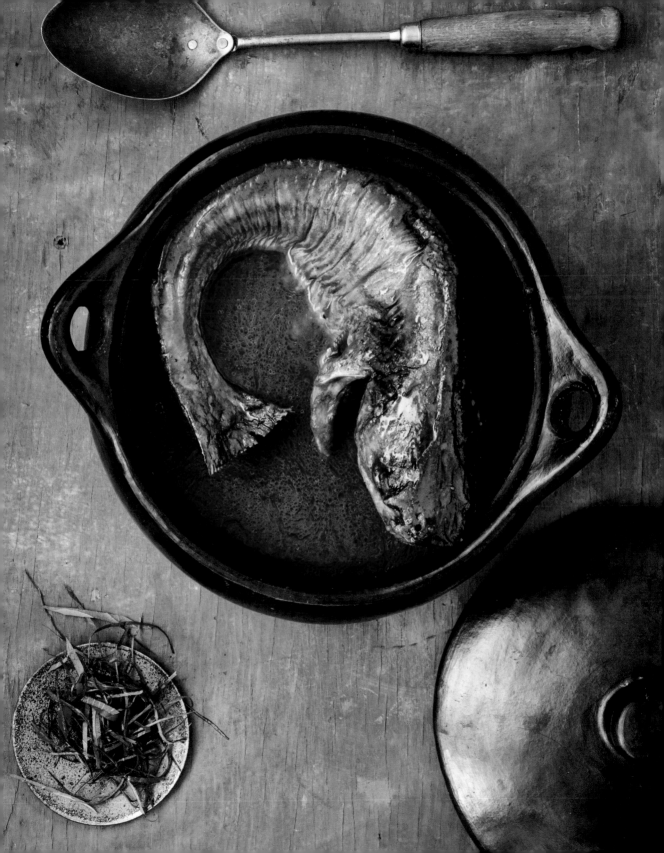

Ọbẹ̀ is the Yorùbá word for stew. It's our flavorful, sometimes fiery base sauce for coaxing the tenderness out of braising meats, or slow-simmering fish or vegetables. It has a long history in our cuisine and was typically cooked to be used day-of when refrigeration wasn't an option.

Tangy with a lingering heat from the mix of bell peppers, tomatoes, and chiles, the sauce perfectly balances bright acidic flavors with a spicy bite. In this recipe, a smoked guinea hen serves as the sauce's brilliant foil, adding a layer of richness. This is reminiscent of those yard bird dinners I had growing up: a chicken fresh from our backyard cooked over an open flame, smoke from the woodfire lingering in the hot night air.

Ọbẹ̀ is best served over steamed rice and a side of fried sweet plantains, or as the accompanying stew with any of the soups.

Ọbẹ̀ WITH SMOKED GUINEA HEN

SERVES 4

2 to 3 pounds smoked bone-in guinea hen parts, cut into 2-inch pieces, or 1 pound cooked meat, such as beef, goat, or lamb

2 tablespoons neutral oil such as grapeseed or canola

2 cups Ata Lílọ̀ (page 90)

2 cups chicken stock (page 79)

Fine salt to taste

Steamed rice and Dòdò (fried sweet plantains, page 193) or Òkèlè (page 52), for serving

In a small pot, pour cold water over the smoked hen parts and place over medium heat. Bring to a boil and allow to simmer for 10 minutes. Pour out the water, rinse the hen parts, and replace with cold water. Repeat the simmer and rinse steps at least two more times to rehydrate and rinse of any excess salt used to preserve the hen. You can do this step ahead and store the boiled hen refrigerated in a sealed container for up to 48 hours.

In a large pot, heat the oil over medium heat. Add the ata lílọ̀ and stock and bring to a boil. Season lightly with salt. Transfer the hen parts to the stew pot and reduce the heat to low. Cover and simmer, stirring frequently until the hen parts are softened through and tender, 25 to 30 minutes. Season to taste with additional salt.

Serve the stew hot over rice with a nice side of dòdò or any of the òkèlè.

Growing up, this was the ultimate market day soup. A bounty of fresh ingredients would be laid out on the counter when we got home to be washed, inspected, and prepped for their path to the pot. My siblings and I would sit on little stools in the kitchen, picking the ègúsí seeds from their shells. It was a chore, but we knew a delicious reward awaited us.

There are much more convenient means of making ègúsí soup. The seeds can be bought shelled, and the stew base is a step to complete ahead. I have learned to approach the task with a delicate hand: I stir as little as possible while the soup is cooking because doing so encourages the ground seeds to clump up. With a light touch, this soup rewards you with a riot of flavor and textures.

Ègúsí Soup

SERVES 4

1 cup shelled ègúsí seeds

Fine salt to taste

2 cups Ata Gígé (page 89)

¼ cup red palm oil

1 pound cooked meat or roast mushrooms (see page 166)

2 pounds mature spinach, stemmed, blanched, and squeezed dry (about 4 cups after squeezing)

Puree the ègúsí seeds in a blender or food processor with water and a pinch of fine sea salt until a smooth paste is formed. Set aside.

Add the ata gígé into a large saucepan and heat up gently over medium heat. Allow to come to a simmer, stirring frequently. Reduce the heat to medium low and add your blended ègúsí paste in tablespoon-sized clumps. Add the red palm oil. Cover the soup and allow the paste to cook without stirring the stew, about 6 minutes.

Add the meat or mushrooms and the drained leafy greens, stir, and cook until warmed through. Adjust the seasoning with salt and remove from the heat.

Serve over steamed rice or any of the swallows from page 52.

NOTE Full of healthy fats, ègúsí seeds are the nutritious and filling base ingredient for this soup. Ègúsí seeds are a great source of protein, so this soup can be served with or without meat. Raw, shelled pumpkin seeds will make an adequate substitute if ègúsí seeds are not available.

This brothy soup is made from a distinct blend of ground seeds, spices, chiles, and fresh herbs. For me, peppersoup embodies the playfulness and inventiveness of our cuisine. The delicate layering of flavors is a hallmark of so many of our best dishes. One generous spoonful of this heady broth is all it takes to feel the sensation of sweat sweeping over you and a sharp tingling flare in your nostrils—exactly what you'd experience in the humidity of noontime Lagos. While whole cuts of bone-in meats are essential to the broth, a lively mix of mushrooms will make for a satisfactory vegetarian version. Fresh scent leaf is the ideal finish, but in its absence any herb with a sharp bite, such as basil or cilantro, will work.

Peppersoup WITH SHORT RIBS

SERVES 6 TO 8

3½ to 4 pounds bone-in short ribs, cut into 4-inch pieces

2 large red onions (about 1½ pounds), peeled and quartered

1 (2-inch) piece of ginger, scrubbed and thinly sliced

2 stalks of lemongrass, cut into 4-inch pieces and smashed with the back of a knife

1 garlic bulb, halved crosswise

1 fresh bay leaf

6 small dried hot chiles, such as bird's-eye or cayenne

2 dried smoked chiles, such as chipotle

6 selim seed pods (optional), crushed lightly using the back of a knife

1 tablespoon Trinity Pepper Paste (page 102)

10 sprigs fresh thyme

1 small bunch of parsley

1 small bunch of cilantro

2 tablespoons Toasted Peppersoup Spice (page 99), plus more for garnish

Fine salt to taste

¼ cup fresh mint leaves

¼ cup picked scent leaves (or African or Thai basil)

Place the short ribs in a stockpot and cover with about 4 quarts of water. Add in the onions, ginger, lemongrass, garlic, bay leaf, dried chiles, and selim seed pods if using. Place over high heat, bring up to a boil and lower the heat to medium. Allow the stock to simmer until the meat is cooked through, tender, and falls apart when picked at with a fork, about 2½ to 3 hours. Add more water as needed to keep the liquid 2 inches above the surface of the meat. Remove the short ribs, set aside, and add the pepper paste, thyme, parsley, and cilantro.

While the stock is simmering, toast and grind your peppersoup spice if making your own. Skip this step if using store-bought ground spice blend.

Strain out all the vegetable solids and return the stock to the pot. Add in the peppersoup spice, season with salt, and bring up to a boil over high heat. Reduce the heat to low and allow the broth to simmer. Return the short ribs to the pot and simmer on low until the meat is fork tender, 30 minutes.

Divide the soup into bowls. Serve topped with the fresh mint and scent leaves and an additional sprinkling of the peppersoup spice. You can enjoy this fiery soup by itself or serve alongside steamed white rice, boiled plantains, or slices of Agége Bread (page 115) if you like.

VEGETABLE SOUPS

Most anglophone West Africans will refer to a dish containing a combination of vegetables, fish and/or meat cooked in a liquid as a "soup" or a "stew." Technically speaking, it's a very fine line that differentiates a soup from a stew. The soup recipes you see throughout this book are *not* going to result in a pot of steaming hot broth with toppings. With very few exceptions, like Peppersoup on page 175, you'll find that our vegetable soups are not very watery, nor are they served alone.

Nigerian soups are always intended to be paired with grains or starches for smothering or dipping, sometimes even layered with another soup or stew.

Every region of Nigeria has several versions of stewed greens, in which the greens are combined with flavorful pantry items to create a complex and delicious soup. This is by no means a definitive list of vegetable soups. The few highlighted here are some of my favorites, ones I return to. For me, making one of these soups always starts with a visit to the market, picking out the freshest of greens from endless leafy piles, and planning a whole meal around them. While they are often considered sides or accompaniments, they are perfect served with or without starches or swallows.

Known as onugbu in Igbo, ewúró in Yorùbá, and shiwaka in Hausa, bitterleaf is a culinary and medicinal herb native to sub-Saharan Africa. Mashed or pureed cocoyam and palm oil are the starch and fat, respectively, and work together to temper the bitterness of the greens. I leave the starch as tender crushed pieces for a chunky consistency for this soup, but it's quite common to have the cocoyam swirled in as a pureed paste, thickening the broth as it dissolves. Serve this soup with any of the swallows from pages 52–55. If you want to add meat, you can simply season and cook it in advance.

Ofe Onugbu
(Bitterleaf Soup with Cocoyam)

SERVES 4

1 pound white cocoyam (taro root) or white sweet potatoes

Fine salt to taste

6 cups meat or chicken stock (page 79) or vegetable stock or water

1 pound cooked meat, such as beef, goat, or lamb

1 cup loosely packed rehydrated stockfish flakes (see page 75, optional)

1 tablespoon Trinity Pepper Paste (page 102)

2 tablespoons red palm oil

2 cups packed washed fresh bitterleaf or chopped dandelion greens (or use 1 cup rehydrated bitter leaves)

Swallow, such as àmàlà, èbà (see headnote, page 49), or tuwo (page 56), for serving

Remove the brown skin on the root by peeling off with a paring knife or a vegetable peeler. Move the peeled roots to a bowl of water to keep from oxidizing. Rinse off the pieces and place in a medium saucepan. Cover with water and bring to a boil over medium-high heat. Season with salt and reduce heat to a simmer. Allow the cocoyam to cook until completely softened, about 10 minutes.

Drain off any remaining liquid and move the cocoyam to a bowl. Once cooled enough to handle, crush the cocoyam into smaller pieces using your fingers or the back of a fork. Cover and set aside.

Bring the stock up to a simmer in a large pot set over medium-high heat. Add any cooked meat pieces, if using. Add softened dried fish pieces if using, and the trinity pepper paste. Stir and simmer until the meat is warmed through and the fish is tender, about 10 minutes. Cook further until the liquid is reduced to about three-quarters of the original volume.

Stir in the red palm oil. Reduce the heat to medium. Using a whisk, stir in ¼ cup of the crushed cocoyam. Whisk vigorously to break up the crushed pieces and mix them into the sauce. The sauce should begin to thicken. Stir in enough of the cocoyam to thicken the sauce so it coats a spoon without running off—you will need ¾ cup to 1 cup of the crushed yam.

Stir in the bitterleaf and cook until warmed through. Adjust the seasoning with more salt if necessary. Ladle the soup into bowls and serve warm alone or with a swallow for a satisfying meal.

NOTE Bitterleaves are a staple vegetable across equatorial Africa. They impart a craveable hint of bitterness to vegetable soups or stews and work much like most herbs used to accent a dish. The fresh leaves get rubbed with salt and rinsed repeatedly before use so all that remains is a slightly bitter note. Such plants have offered us a versatility of flavor and function, shaping our palates and supporting our health for centuries.

Among the most popular dishes in Nigeria, and especially among people in Cross River and Akwa Ibom States, edika ikong is something I tried for the first time in Brooklyn of all places, at a restaurant on Fulton Street aptly named Buka. The unmistakable flavors of our essential ingredients—palm oil, hot chiles, and dried seafood are prominent in this soup. The classic version of edika ikong is a rich soup composed of braised ugwu leaves with tender waterleaf folded in, but the base sauce is endlessly adaptable. Go with a green that can withstand a simmer such as collards and pair it with a softer green such as mature spinach. Typically served with a swallow, edika ikong is also lovely over a bowl of steamed rice.

Edika Ikong (Ugwu and Waterleaf Soup)

SERVES 4

Fine salt to taste

1 pound fresh ugwu leaves or any hearty green such as collards, kale, beet, or turnip

1 pound fresh gbúre (waterleaf) leaves or any tender green such as mature spinach

2 tablespoons red palm oil

1 medium yellow onion, peeled and chopped

1 to 2 tablespoons Trinity Pepper Paste (page 102)

2 cups meat or chicken stock (page 79) or vegetable stock

8 to 10 ounces cooked meat or mushrooms (see page 166), optional

Òkèlè (page 52) or swallow (page 52), for serving

Bring a large pot of salted water to a boil over high heat. Working in batches, blanch the leaves quickly, starting with the ugwu. Drop the ugwu leaves into the water, stir, and cook until just bright green and tender, 1 to 2 minutes. Drain out the liquid and run the cooked leaves under cold water or transfer to a bowl of water filled with ice. Repeat the blanching step with the gbúre leaves, cooking for a minute until just wilted. Drain and set both sets of leaves aside.

In a medium-size Dutch oven, heat the palm oil over medium heat. Add the onion and sauté until just softened, about 3 minutes. Add the pepper paste and cook until fragrant, about 1 minute. Add the stock and any cooked meats or mushrooms, if using. Bring the brothy liquid up to a simmer and allow to reduce slightly, about 3 minutes. Season with salt.

Fold in the blanched ugwu leaves and allow to cook until just tender, 5 to 6 minutes. Add the blanched gbúre leaves and cook until warmed through, about 2 minutes. Taste and adjust seasoning with salt. Serve the edika ikong warm with any type of òkèlè or swallow.

This soup features kuka, the powdered leaves of the baobab fruit tree. Available as a coarse or fine powder, kuka acts as a thickener for the brothy, meaty base. It's not often that I find baobab leaf powder here, so I use moringa leaf powder, an adequate substitution. Be sure to serve this northern Nigerian soup with something filling, such as Funkaso (page 200) or any swallow. Traditionally, it is served alongside Tuwo Shinkafa (page 56) for a complete and satisfying meal.

Miyan Kuka (Baobab Leaf Soup)

SERVES 4

2 tablespoons red palm oil

1 small onion, minced

1 tablespoon Trinity Pepper Paste (page 102)

6 cups meat or chicken stock (page 79) or vegetable stock

¼ cup baobab leaf powder (kuka) or moringa leaf powder

1 tablespoon ground dawadawa powder

Fine salt to taste

1 pound cooked meat, chicken, seafood or roast mixed mushrooms (page 166)

2 cups Ata Dín Dín (page 93), Ọbẹ̀ with Smoked Guinea Hen (page 171), or Ofada Stew (page 220), for serving

Tuwo Shinkafa (page 56), for serving

In a large pot, heat the oil over medium heat. Add the onion and sauté until softened and translucent, about 5 minutes. Add the pepper paste and sauté until just fragrant, about 1 minute. Stir in the stock. Bring to a boil and lower to a simmer until the flavors meld, the broth reduces slightly, and oil begins to rise to the surface, about 12 minutes.

Reduce the heat to low and whisk in the baobab leaf powder. Stir vigorously to dissolve. Add the dawadawa powder and allow to simmer until the sauce is reduced, about three-quarters of the original volume. Season with salt to taste.

Add the cooked meat or seafood, if using, and cook until warmed through. Remove from heat and season with additional salt if necessary.

Ladle in shallow bowls and top with ata, ọbẹ̀, or ofada stew. Serve with tuwo shinkafa swallows.

Sorrel is one of the greens I source from my friend Yemi's Oko Farms. Commonly referred to as yakwa or yakuwa in Hausa, I've used these hearty, lemony greens generously in salads, stirred them into broths, and sprinkled them as a garnish for the braised goat (page 223) course at my dinners. I'm entranced by its bright, tangy zing, and this soup is its perfect showcase.

Chopping, blanching, and squeezing dry the sorrel before adding it to the base of fermented locust bean and chiles will intensify their flavor. Tuwo shinkafa provides a neutral counterpoint for this soup, but funkaso or sinasir will also help soak up Miyan Yakuwa's delicious complexity.

Miyan Yakuwa (Sorrel Soup)

SERVES 4

2 bunches of yakuwa (lemon sorrel), about 1 pound/ 453 grams

2 tablespoons toasted peanut oil

1 small onion, chopped

1 tablespoon grated fresh ginger

1 teaspoon ground dawadawa powder

1 teaspoon chile powder (such as cayenne)

4 cups chopped fresh tomatoes or one 14.5-ounce can whole peeled tomatoes

Fine salt to taste

2 tablespoons red palm oil

Tuwo shinkafa (see page 56), Funkaso (page 200), or Sinasir (page 204), for serving

Bring a large pot of water to a boil over high heat. Working in batches if you need to, blanch the yakuwa leaves quickly until just bright green and tender, about 1 minute. Drain out and run the cooked leaves under cold water or transfer to a bowl of water filled with ice. Set aside.

In a large saucepan over medium heat, heat the peanut oil. Add the onion and sauté until softened. Add the ginger, dawadawa powder, and chile powder and toast until fragrant, about 1 minute. Add the tomatoes, plus any juice, and use a wooden spoon to stir and break the tomatoes up

into smaller pieces as needed. Allow the tomatoes to simmer and reduce into a jammy sauce. Season with salt to taste.

Drain the liquid from the yakuwa leaves and squeeze out any excess using your hands. Once the sauce is reduced, stir in the yakuwa leaves and cook until warmed through, about 5 minutes. Stir in the palm oil and allow to cook for another minute or two. Adjust the seasoning.

Transfer the soup to individual bowls and serve warm alongside balls of tuwo shinkafa, funkaso, or sinasir.

This is a wonderfully simple soup of oha leaves thickened by cooked and pureed roots or tubers. In other variations, ground seeds such as achi, offor, or cocoyam powder are used as thickeners. Oha leaves can be found at most markets when they are in season. At their peak, they are sweet and grassy with a tinge of citrus, giving the soup its special character. I love this soup on its own but Ofe Oha, as it is called in Igbo, is equally wonderful when prepared with meat and served with èbà (see headnote, page 49).

I've timed trips to Nigeria around certain growing seasons in order to make the best soups and stews while I'm there. Getting oha leaves fresh will ensure your soup is dazzling. Still, I've wanted my ofe oha in Brooklyn too, so I bring back a bag of leaves that I've dried in the sun during my visit to rehydrate when I'm ready to use them.

Oha Soup

SERVES 4

2 pounds cocoyam (white taro root)

Fine salt to taste

6 cups meat or chicken stock (page 79) or vegetable stock

1 cup loosely packed smoked catfish flakes (page 75, optional)

1 tablespoon Trinity Pepper Paste (page 102)

¼ cup red palm oil

2 cups fresh oha leaves (or use 3 cups dried leaves and rehydrate)

Remove the brown skin on the roots by peeling off with a paring knife or a vegetable peeler. Move the peeled roots to a bowl of water to keep from oxidizing. Rinse off the pieces and place in a medium saucepan. Cover with water and bring to a boil over medium-high heat. Season with salt and reduce heat to a simmer. Allow the cocoyam to cook until completely softened, about 10 minutes.

Drain off any remaining liquid and move the cocoyam to a bowl. Once cooled enough to handle, crush it into smaller pieces using your fingers or the back of a fork. Cover and set aside.

Bring the stock to a simmer in a large pot set over medium-high heat. Stir in the smoked fish pieces, if using, and pepper paste. Allow to simmer until the liquid is reduced to about three-quarters of its original volume. Strain the stock through a fine-mesh sieve to remove and discard the solids.

Using a blender, carefully puree 2 cups of the stock mixture with the crushed cocoyam pieces until smooth. Return the mixture back to the pot with the rest of the stock. Stir in the red palm oil. Using a wooden spoon, stir the soup while cooking over low heat.

Stir in the oha leaves and adjust the seasoning with more salt if necessary. Cook until warmed through and beginning to simmer, 4 to 5 minutes. Ladle the soup into bowls and serve warm.

SIDES

These delicious side dishes will bring variety, fun, and pops of color to your plate. They all pair well with other dishes and in some cases are meant to be functional—plates of fluffy sinasir or funkaso are your convenient vehicles for soups and stews. Sweet plantains paired with spicy dishes will temper the bite from the chiles. The bean dishes are yours to play with, pair with rice, or enjoy with a cold bowl of soaked garri and peanuts. From abacha, burabisco, dan wake to nkwobi, these sides are all composed to delight or hold their own as a snack/light nosh.

Abacha is essentially a fresh salad of shaved, blanched cassava pieces coated in a rich sauce of ucha and tossed with scent leaves. This version adds lime and cilantro for a little sparkle.

Abacha

**YIELD: 4 TO 6 SERVINGS
(ABOUT 6 CUPS)**

Fine salt to taste

2½ pounds
cassava root
(about 2 whole)

½ teaspoon kaun
or baking soda

½ cup red palm oil

1 teaspoon Trinity
Pepper Paste
(page 102)

1 cup fresh herbs
such as efirin,
cilantro, and mint

1 small red onion,
thinly sliced and
soaked in cold
water

Lime slices, for
squeezing

Bring a medium pot of generously salted water to a boil.

Remove the skin on the cassava roots by peeling with a paring knife or a vegetable peeler. Move the peeled roots to a bowl of water to keep them from turning brown.

Using the large side of a box grater, grate the peeled cassava pieces into the bowl of water to keep the starch from oxidizing. Blanch the grated cassava in the boiling water for 1 minute, drain and run immediately under cold water. Spread out on a kitchen towel to dry and cool completely.

In a small bowl, combine the kaun with 2 tablespoons water. Pour the palm oil in a large mixing bowl and whisk in the kaun mixture until the oil begins to curdle. Stir in the pepper paste breaking up the paste with the whisk to incorporate. Season with salt. Gently fold in the blanched cassava pieces. Taste and adjust the seasoning if necessary.

Chop half of the herbs and stir into the salad with half of the onion. Transfer to a serving bowl or individual plates. Garnish with the remaining herbs, sliced onion, and slices of lime for squeezing.

This is a wonderful and effortless side that works best with soft-skinned beans like honey beans, black-eyed peas, yellow-eyed peas, or pinto beans, but any bean varieties you have on hand will work well. The onions melt and lend their aromatic essence to the body of the cooked beans as they are mashed in the pot.

Ẹ̀wà Sísè (Cooked Mashed Beans)

YIELD: 4 CUPS

2 cups dried ẹ̀wà olóyin or dried beans such as black-eyed peas, yellow-eyed peas, or pintos, soaked 4 to 12 hours

1 red onion, peeled, diced

Fine salt to taste

Drain the beans and place in a large pot. Add water to cover by 3 to 4 inches. Bring to a boil over high heat and lower to a simmer. Cook uncovered, adding more water as necessary to keep from drying out, until the beans are tender and soft but not falling apart, about 50 minutes.

Add in the chopped onion, season with salt and cook until the onions are softened, about 10 minutes. Allow the beans to cool slightly. Drain out any excess liquid. Mash the beans to a coarse puree with the back of a wooden spoon or a potato masher.

Serve the mashed beans hot, topped with Ata Dín Dín (page 93), with sides such as Dòdò (page 193), or with any of the boiled starches from pages 59-60.

Ẹ̀wà Agoyin has its roots in Beninese and Togolese cuisines and has become a staple on buka menus across Lagos. Honey beans, cooked until soft enough to crush with a fork, are combined with onions and crayfish to build a mix of essential flavors: a little sweetness, a little salt, and a nice balance of umami. The potent flavor profile of the Agoyin Sauce (see page 94) is the real star here. Serve in shallow bowls with the sauce pooled in the center or stirred in and alongside thick slices of agége bread for dipping.

Ẹ̀wà Agoyin

**YIELD: 4 TO
6 SERVINGS
(ABOUT 5 CUPS)**

1 cup Agoyin
Sauce (page 94),
warmed

4 cups Ẹ̀wà
Sísè (opposite),
warmed

Garri, for serving

Agége Bread
(page 115),
for serving

Serve the agoyin sauce spooned over a
bowl of warm ẹ̀wà sísè (warm cooked
beans) with a side of garri for sprinkling
and thick slices of agége bread.

Ẹ̀wà ríró is the Yorùbá name for a creamy bean dish that features
palm oil stirred into cooked honey beans. It can be a main dish or
a side. It's also the beans of "beans and dòdò" and a go-to dish for
casual weekday meals in my home. The lovely richness of crayfish
and spices also give the dish its distinctive flavor.

Ẹ̀wà Ríró

**YIELD: 4 TO 6 SERVINGS
(ABOUT 5 CUPS COOKED BEANS)**

2 teaspoons
neutral oil such as
grapeseed

1 red onion, diced

¼ cup whole dried
crayfish, soaked in
warm water

1 tablespoon
tomato paste

2 cups Ata Dín Dín
(page 93)

Fine salt to taste

4 cups Ẹ̀wà Sísè
(opposite)

¼ cup red palm oil

¼ cup garri, for
sprinkling

Dòdò (fried
sweet plantains,
page 193), for
serving

2 green onions,
trimmed and thinly
sliced (optional),
for serving

In a large saucepan, heat the
oil over medium heat and
add the onion. Sauté the
onion until softened and just
beginning to brown, about
8 minutes. Drain the crayfish
and add it to the onion. Cook
until fragrant, about 2 minutes. Add the tomato paste
and cook until it darkens,
about 2 minutes.

Pour in the ata dín dín, stirring to loosen any bits stuck
to the bottom. Bring to a boil
and lower to a simmer. Allow
the sauce to cook, stirring frequently until it thickens, and
the oil rises to the top, about
20 minutes. Season with salt

to taste. You should have about
2 cups sauce.

Add the ẹ̀wà sísè (cooked
beans) and stir to combine.
Simmer the beans in the sauce
until the sauce thickens and
the flavors begin to meld, 12 to
15 minutes. Add the palm oil,
season with more salt if necessary, and cook for an additional
5 minutes.

Serve the bowls of warm ẹ̀wà
ríró topped with garri and
plenty of dòdò. Garnish with
sliced green onions, if desired.

This is a warm, filling one-pot bean dish, enlivened by the addition of fresh corn (but frozen corn will work in a pinch). The smoked fish lends it additional umami, the pepper paste a lingering heat, and the palm oil creaminess. To keep this vegetarian, simply omit the smoked fish or replace it with sautéed mushrooms. Serve adalu warm, topped with a scattering of fresh herbs and alongside fried sweet plantains.

Adalu

**YIELD:
4 SERVINGS
(ABOUT 5 CUPS
COOKED BEANS)**

2 teaspoons neutral oil such as grapeseed

1 red onion, diced

1 tablespoon Trinity Pepper Paste (page 102)

1 cup Ata Lílò (page 90)

Fine salt to taste

2 cups Èwà Sísè (page 58)

2 cups fresh or frozen corn kernels

1 cup smoked fish fillets, skin and bones removed, fillets broken into 1- to 2-inch pieces

¼ cup red palm oil

¼ cup scent leaf, julienned, for serving

¼ cup garri, for sprinkling

Dòdò (fried sweet plantains, opposite), for serving

In a large pot, heat the grapeseed oil over medium heat and add the onion. Sauté the onion until softened and just beginning to brown, about 8 minutes. Add the pepper paste. Cook until fragrant, about 2 minutes. Pour in the ata lílò, stirring to loosen any bits stuck to the bottom. Bring to a boil and lower to a simmer. Allow the sauce to cook, stirring frequently until it thickens and the oil rises to the top, about 10 minutes. Season with salt to taste.

Add the èwà sísè and stir to combine. Simmer the beans in the sauce until the sauce thickens and flavors begin to meld, 12 to 15 minutes.

Add the corn, smoked fish pieces, and palm oil, season with more salt if necessary, and cook for an additional 5 minutes. Serve the adalu warm topped with scent leaves. Sprinkle with garri and serve alongside plenty of dòdò.

NOTE Èwà àsepò is the Yorùbá name for any one-pot meal of beans and a starchy vegetable cooked together. Adalu is a type of àsepò, and the ratio here can be adjusted for any other starch. Èwà àsepò is typically served as a main dish and is quite filling on its own. Yams, sweet potatoes, and cocoyam are examples of starches used in èwà àsepò recipes. To make èwà àsepò with any of these ingredients, peel one pound of the starchy vegetables of your choice and cut into 1-inch pieces. Replace the corn in this recipe with the diced starchy vegetables. Add in a cup of stock or water and cook until tender and the sauce is thickened. Continue with step 3 above and serve warm, topped with a sprinkling of garri and fresh herbs.

Dòdò, as it is called in Yorùbá, refers to the fried preparation of ripened plantains. The cut of the plantain determines its place at the table. Nice thick slices on the bias are typically served as a main with stewed meat, while smaller diced cubes or rounds can be paired with any sauce, stew, or side dish. My mother keeps a large plastic tub of fried sweet plantains in the freezer, reheating a batch for dinner whenever she craves them.

I enjoy my fried sweet plantains tostones-style: twice-fried and from the ripest plantains in the house. Twice-frying is not traditional, but the thicker, evenly caramelized sweet crust is worth the additional step in my opinion. The traditional or once-fried method below still gives them a nice, sweet crust and a meatier middle. An even brown color is ideal, so patience is the name of the game here.

Dòdò
(Fried Sweet Plantains)

SERVES 4 TO 6

4 yellow or spotted black and yellow medium plantains (about 2¼ pounds)

Canola or other neutral oil, for frying

Fine salt to taste

Peel the plantains by using a sharp knife to make a slit in the skin (avoid cutting the flesh) down the middle, and remove the skin by peeling back with your hands. Cut off the tip at both ends. Cut the plantain crosswise on a diagonal into thick 1-inch pieces.

In a large sauté pan, pour enough oil to cover up to ½ inch from the bottom. Heat the oil over medium heat.

Working in batches, fry the plantain pieces, turning once, until they are a light golden brown across the surface and caramelized around the edges, 10 to 12 minutes. Remove plantains from the oil and drain on a wire rack or a plate set with paper towels.

Toss the golden brown pieces of fried plantains with a pinch of salt. Serve warm or at room temperature.

NOTE: PICKING PLANTAINS The plantains used here should be yellow or speckled with large black dots. Depending on your preference, you can certainly use black plantains which will be on the high end of the sweet spectrum, just know that some sections may absorb more oil. If you can only find green plantains, you will have to be patient. Pop them in a brown paper bag, fold down the top, and allow them to sit for 2 to 3 days to ripen to the spotted yellow color needed.

Burabisco is a preparation of dried cassava rehydrated with a stock or water. It is reminiscent of fluffy clumps of cooked couscous, and has its roots in the former Bornu Empire from which the Borno State in northeastern Nigeria was carved.

Burabisco works well as a base for a salad. This recipe enlivens the burabisco with fresh ingredients and herbs. Swap out the blistered corn for any vegetables you have on hand; eggplant or roasted pumpkin make adequate substitutes.

Burabisco
WITH BLISTERED SWEET CORN, CUCUMBERS, AND AVOCADOS

SERVES 4

1 cup garri

1 cup warm vegetable stock or water

Fine salt to taste

2 tablespoons Manshanu (page 96)

2 cups corn kernels (about 2 ears)

Juice and zest of 2 limes

1 tablespoon honey

1 pound English cucumbers, cut lengthwise into ½-inch spears, then crosswise into 2-inch pieces

1 avocado, pit removed, flesh quartered

1 packed cup mint leaves

In a medium bowl, combine the garri and warm stock. Use your fingers or a fork to fluff the grains until the liquid is absorbed and you end up with pebble-size clumps of garri. Season with salt, cover, and set the burabisco aside.

In a small saucepan, melt the manshanu over medium-high heat. Add the corn kernels and cook without stirring, allowing the kernels to blister slightly, 3 to 4 minutes. Season with salt and fold the corn into the burabisco.

Whisk together the lime juice, zest, and honey in a small bowl.

Divide the burabisco mixture among shallow bowls. Top each bowl with a quarter of the cucumber pieces and a quarter of the avocado. Spoon the dressing over the top and finish with a handful of mint leaves. Serve immediately.

Frejon, cooked beans pureed with coconut milk, is an ode to the rich history and cultural diversity of the coastal city of Lagos. Frejon is thought to have originated in Brazil and was brought back by formerly enslaved and repatriated returnees who settled heavily on Lagos Island. Afro-Brazilian influences suffuse so much of Lagos's cultural life: everything from food and architecture to agriculture and religion. As I was growing up, this dish was especially significant during the Christian Holy Week leading up to Easter. Primarily served on Good Friday, my maternal grandmother—who practiced a fluid mix of both Christian and Islamic holiday traditions—would make a batch of frejon to send out to family members.

Frejon is relatively easy to make and can be accompanied by a fish stew (page 232), Ata Dín Dín (page 93), or any stewed protein. A sprinkling of dry garri is traditional and adds some texture.

Frejon

SERVES 4 TO 6

2 cups dried èwà olóyin, black-eyed peas, or pinto beans

1 small bunch of fresh thyme (about 10 sprigs)

1 yellow onion, halved

1 bay leaf

Fine salt to taste

1 cup unsweetened coconut milk, plus more if needed

Ata Dín Dín (page 93), for serving

¼ cup garri, for sprinkling

Pick through the beans for rocks, bad grains, or twigs. Place the beans in a large bowl with water up to 2 inches above the surface and allow to soak for 4 hours to overnight. Drain and rinse the beans and move to a medium pot. Cover with water up to 2 inches above the surface.

Wrap the thyme, half the onion, and the bay leaf in a piece of cheesecloth tied with twine. Add to the pot and bring to a boil. Reduce to a simmer and allow to cook on low, partly covered with a lid, until the beans are completely tender, about 1½ hours. Season with salt and allow the beans to cool slightly in cooking liquid. Remove the aromatics.

Drain the beans out of the liquid and place in a food processor. Pour in the coconut milk and pulse to a coarse puree. Use more coconut milk for a smooth puree, or less for a thicker, puree if you prefer. Pour the puree back into the pot and keep warm on low heat stirring occasionally to keep the bottom from scorching.

Serve warm alongside ata dín dín or other stews, with garri for sprinkling.

This fritter is a gift to dipping sauces, acting as the perfect vessel to scoop up flavor and sop up sauces and stews. Of course there are many variations, including a few versions jazzed up with chopped onions in the batter. I like using whole wheat flour, but millet flour is traditionally used in Nigeria and substitutes well here.

Funkaso (Whole Wheat Fritters)

SERVES 6

1½ cups lukewarm water, about 110°F

1 tablespoon active dry yeast

2½ cups whole wheat flour

1½ teaspoons fine sea salt

4 cups peanut oil, for frying

In a small bowl, whisk together the water and yeast and allow to sit until foamy, about 6 minutes.

In a medium bowl, sift together the whole wheat flour and salt. Make a well in the center and pour in the yeast mixture. Combine, stirring with a wooden spoon to incorporate the ingredients. The batter should be smooth and slightly loose, similar to the puff puff batter (see page 147).

Cover the bowl with a kitchen towel and allow to rise until doubled in size.

Heat the oil over medium-high heat until it shimmers. Dip your fingers into a bowl of water and pinch off a tablespoon-size piece of the batter. Use your thumb to poke a hole in the middle of the piece as you carefully drop the batter into the hot oil. Repeat the steps of wetting your fingers each time you drop a piece of the batter into the oil. Drop enough pieces in the oil to fill the pan but still have room to turn the batter. Fry the funkaso, turning frequently until they are a nice golden brown color all over, 4 to 5 minutes. Transfer the fried pieces to a cooling rack or plate lined with paper towels to cool. Working in batches, fry the remaining batter.

Serve the funkaso alone or alongside stews such as Miyan Taushe (page 235), Miyan Kuka (page 181), Gbègìrì (page 203), or any of the èwà dishes.

Known as gbẹ̀gìrì in Yorùbá and miyan wakye in Hausa, this bean soup delights in its simplicity. Onions, crayfish, and palm oil make for a straightforward set of ingredients; the real commitment comes from pureeing the soup itself. In Lagos, it's often served as a trio of multicolored complements called abula consisting of àmàlà, gbẹ̀gìrì, and ewédú, topped with ọbẹ̀ or ata dín dín. It's a visually striking presentation in a single bowl. On its own, gbẹ̀gìrì is comfort food exemplified.

Gbẹ̀gìrì

SERVES 4

¼ cup red palm oil

1 small onion, chopped

1 Scotch bonnet pepper, stemmed

4 garlic cloves

1-inch piece of ginger, scrubbed

1 tablespoon ground dried crayfish

2 cups dried peeled beans (see note), such as honey beans, black-eyed peas, or peeled mung beans, rinsed and drained

In a medium saucepan, warm the oil over medium heat and sauté the onion until translucent. Add the Scotch bonnet pepper, garlic, ginger, and crayfish. Sauté until just fragrant, about 2 minutes. Add the peeled beans and enough water to cover up to 2 inches above the top. Stir and bring to a boil over high heat, then reduce to a simmer.

Cook until the beans are completely tender and falling apart into the sauce, adding in more water if necessary—it should look like a chunky soup at this point. Remove from the heat and allow to cool slightly. Move the soup to a blender, puree with 1 cup of water until smooth, and return the soup to the pot. Serve immediately or keep the soup warm over low heat.

NOTE If using unpeeled beans, soak ahead for 4 hours and up to 12 hours. Peel the beans by sliding them together using both hands. The skins should float to the top of the liquid and you can pour off and discard them. Repeat this process until the beans are mostly all peeled.

Beans can be purchased peeled, but if you cannot locate them and you do not peel your beans in advance, you can always strain the pureed bean mixture through a fine strainer.

This flat skillet cake is made from a fermented rice paste with a spongy consistency and texture reminiscent of Somalian cambabuur, South Indian dosas, and Ethiopian injera.

Sinasir is a feast for the senses. The lovely fragrance of toasted rice is accompanied by an even lovelier texture of a crackly exterior with a moist interior. It liberally soaks up stews and sauces, and is a divine snack when drizzled in local honey.

Sinasir

YIELD: 8 SINASIR

1 teaspoon yeast

2 cups Fermented Rice Paste (page 41)

2 teaspoons fine sea salt

¼ cup Manshanu (page 96)

Honey, for serving

Dissolve the yeast in a small bowl with ¼ cup warm water and set aside. Pour the fermented rice paste into a medium bowl and stir in the salt. Pour the yeast mixture into the paste and salt and mix.

Cover and allow to rise until doubled in size and foamy, about 1 hour (at this point you can also leave the batter to ferment and develop more flavor by letting it rise slowly in the refrigerator over a 12-hour period).

Stir the batter until smooth, making sure to get any paste that has settled along the bottom of the bowl during rising. The batter should coat your spoon or spatula.

Over medium-high heat, warm a well-seasoned small (8-inch) skillet and add a tablespoon of manshanu. Ladle in ½ cup of batter and spread to the edges of the pan. Cook until the surface of the cake is dotted with holes and the edges are crisp golden brown, 3 to 4 minutes.

Use a spatula to loosen the cake from the pan and flip to cook the other side, about 1 minute. Transfer to a plate. Repeat with the remaining batter, adding more manshanu with every new cake. Serve warm, by itself drizzled with honey or alongside Beef Suya (page 141) or soups such as Miyan Taushe (page 235) or Miyan Kuka (page 181).

I can wax poetic about the joys of nkwobi—the way it incorporates ucha, how it can be made with a varying amounts of pepper, its delightfully pungent aroma (seriously, somebody stop me)—but the reality is that it can be a difficult dish to pull off. Get out that pressure cooker to save some time, go to a butcher who can source and cut the cow's foot you'll need, then set aside the day. It takes some serious cooking to break down cow foot, but the rest of the dish comes together easily, and is a uniquely memorable experience.

Nkwobi

SERVES 4

1½ pounds cut cow hooves, cleaned

Fine salt to taste

2 onions, one chopped, one thinly sliced

1 cup Ucha (page 105)

½ cup julienned scent leaves or basil

Place the pieces of cow hooves in a pot and add enough water to cover them by 3 or 4 inches. Bring to a boil over high heat. Once boiling, remove from the heat, discard the water, rinse the pieces, and cover with fresh water. Bring to a boil again and lower the heat to a simmer. Season with salt and add the chopped onion. Cook, adding more water if necessary, until the meat is completely tender and falling off the bone, about 3½ hours. Allow the meat to cool slightly in the broth, about 15 minutes.

Move the cow hooves to a large bowl. Add the ucha and stir to coat evenly with the sauce. Toss in the sliced onions and the scent leaves. Taste and season with additional salt if necessary. Transfer to a bowl and serve immediately.

This northern Nigerian dish is served tossed with a little Manshanu (page 96) and Ground Yaji Spice Blend (page 95) and alongside tomato and onion slices. A ground honey bean flour is traditional, but you can make similar dumplings from chickpea, plantain, yam, or cassava flour.

Dan Wake (Bean Dumplings)

SERVES 4

2 cups bean flour

2 tablespoons ground baobab leaves (kuka) or moringa leaf powder

Fine salt to taste

¼ teaspoon kaun or baking soda

¼ cup Manshanu (page 96)

Ground Yaji Spice Blend (page 95), plus more for sprinkling

Sliced tomatoes and red onion, for serving

Combine the bean flour, ground baobab leaves, and salt in a medium bowl and stir to incorporate. Dissolve the kaun in ½ cup water. (If using baking soda, add directly to the flour mixture without dissolving in water and proceed as follows.) Make a well in the center of the flour and pour in the kaun mixture. Stir with a wooden spoon or your hands into a smooth but elastic dough. Add ½ cup water.

Bring a medium pot of lightly salted water to a boil. Working in batches, scoop the dough with a tablespoon measure or a small dessert spoon and drop each portion into the boiling water. Cook the dumplings in the boiling water until they float to the surface.

Use a slotted spoon to drain and move the dumplings to a medium bowl. Once all the dan wake are cooked, toss them with the manshanu and a few tablespoons of the cooking liquid. Add 2 teaspoons of yaji spice and season with additional salt if needed.

Serve with sliced tomatoes, fresh red onion, and additional yaji spice for sprinkling.

THE WEEKEND: CEREMONIAL FOOD AND OFFERINGS

Food is a cornerstone of every culture's celebrations. I am immensely proud of the way we Nigerians use food as an offering in our gatherings, and how our food has always played a powerful role in our cultural traditions.

Our foods feature prominently in ceremonies that accompany the important highlights of a human's life. Baby-naming ceremonies inspire intricate offerings of ingredients, spices, and provisions. Birthday celebrations, religious observances, weddings, harvest festivals, masquerades, marches, anniversaries, funerals, and remembrances of those who've passed are all filled with rituals expressed through food.

When I moved into a new apartment in the middle of writing this book, I placed onions by the four corners of the house as an offering to Ifa, a Yorùbá deity that watches over those who find themselves in a new space. In my life here in the United States, food continues to be integral to navigating through the phases of growth, change, and adaptation.

I focus on ceremony in the dinners I host. Simple gestures meant to convey welcome, companionship, and gratitude are achieved through the many courses of the meal itself. The host of a Nigerian celebration is no more essential to a gathering than the tables and chairs, or the ingredients that go into the dishes. The real focal point of all Nigerian celebrations is the invited guests.

That's why I've named this chapter "The Weekend." These recipes evoke memories of celebrations and ceremonies that I've attended in Nigeria and abroad. In Lagos, weekends are a time to celebrate holidays and special occasions. Creating some of these dishes is an occasion itself. But the significance of this food is found across the diaspora, and accompanies Nigerians wherever they go.

Time, patience, and of course guests are critical components to the meals featured here. The techniques discussed here are the real treasures of our cuisine, and they are my offering to you. These recipes demand that you get to know the process of Nigerian cuisine very intimately. Time and devotion to the process will certainly yield great—dare I say, divine—results, with practice and repetition. That's because inevitably, the finest dishes of our cuisine have little to do with specific ingredients, but rather how they alchemize with one another, culminating in their own unique offering.

AN OFFERING BOWL

My father always placed spices in a bowl for guests to scoop up with their fingers when they arrived at our home. It was a simple yet significant offering that showed those who we hosted not only that they are welcome, but that there is hope for the evening to follow: that the conversation will flow easily, ideas will be met with open-mindedness and attention, and that the palate is awakened for the exciting flavors to come.

An offering bowl can symbolize many things depending on its contents and this is a tradition I continue in my Brooklyn home.

BABY NAMING OFFERING BOWL

A naming ceremony in Yorùbá culture celebrates the beginning of new life and this is a tradition we decided was important to continue when I had Aṣa and Olamidé. The ceremony is held eight days after the baby is born—the baby is given tiny quantities of specific ingredients that carry symbolic meaning, and the baby's name (typically gifted by older members of the extended family) is announced.

WATER

All Yorùbá ceremonies begin with a cleansing ritual that acknowledges the water deities—Yemọja, Olókun, and Ọ̀ṣun.

HONEY

A little bit of honey on the palate before a conversation is meant to sweeten your conversations with others. Honey is also used as an offering in rituals for joy, blessings, and well wishes including naming ceremonies. A tiny bit of honey is placed on the baby's tongue and a prayer for a sweet life is said for the baby.

ATARE (ALLIGATOR PEPPER)

This spice is used for all initiation rites in ifá ceremonies. It equates to àṣẹ—all prayers are said with atare on the tongue to seal the words/intentions of the prayer. The baby is given a tiny bit to welcome them into the world. Used as the final àṣẹ to seal all of the blessings given to the baby.

KOLA NUT

OBÌ (YORÙBÁ), GWORO (HAUSA); ỌJÌ (IGBO)

Kola nuts are offered to guests in different regions of the country as a welcoming gesture before meetings and gatherings: "ẹni tí o fún ni l'obì loun mu aiye wa fun ni" (the person who brings obi brings life).

In Yorùbá culture, the kola nut has a ubiquitous presence. Whether presented by the basketful to a potential bride's family, shared as a snack amongst friends, or offered to the spirits, obì serves at once as food, medicine, and currency.

BITTER KOLA

ÒRÓGBÓ (YORÙBÁ), MIJI GORO (HAUSA), AKIILU (IGBO)

In Yorùbá culture, bitter kola accompanies prayers for longevity, healing, and spiritual cleansing (Yorùbá). During orìṣà initiations or rituals, òrógbó is used to pray for sound health, longevity, peace, harmony, and happiness.

SALT

Salt embodies the richness of life. Reminiscent of the way the seasoning enhances flavor, it symbolizes the uniqueness of each person.

The success of a batch of jollof rice requires a few key ingredients—a base sauce of ọbẹ ata, herbs, spices, and stock—and a perfect sauce-to-rice ratio (so the cooked grains of rice remain separate). This recipe achieves all of this with very little tending. I have found the best, no fuss way to do this is to make it in the oven.

Because of its increased absorption of flavors, jollof rice is typically made with long-grained parboiled rice, though nonparboiled varieties are my preference and may be interchanged cup for cup. Missing from the oven version is the slightly smoked flavor you get from the little bits of rice that have browned on the bottom of your pan, but that's nothing a pinch of smoked paprika can't fix!

Jollof Rice

SERVES 8 TO 10

½ cup canola or other neutral oil, such as grapeseed or safflower

2 medium red onions, thinly sliced

4 garlic cloves, sliced

1 tablespoon tomato paste

1 teaspoon ground turmeric

2 cups Ata Lílọ (page 90)

3 cups (about 1¼ pounds) parboiled long-grain rice, such as Carolina Gold or Uncle Ben's Original, or any long-grain nonparboiled variety such as basmati or jasmine

5 fresh thyme sprigs

1 fresh bay leaf

Salt and freshly ground black pepper

2 cups meat or chicken stock (page 79) or vegetable stock

Preheat the oven to 350°F. Heat the oil in a large Dutch oven over medium until shimmering, about 1 minute. Add the onions and sauté, stirring frequently until softened, 6 to 8 minutes. Remove half the onions to a plate and set aside. Add the garlic and sauté until fragrant and translucent, about 2 minutes. Add the tomato paste and turmeric and toast until the turmeric is fragrant and tomato paste has deepened to a dark red color, about 2 minutes.

Stir in the ata lílọ and bring to a simmer over medium heat. Stir in the rice, thyme, and bay leaf and season with salt and pepper. Pour in the stock, stir, and cover with a lid. Transfer the pot to the oven and cook until rice is just tender, 35 minutes.

Remove the pot from the oven and allow to sit, covered (no peeking) for 15 minutes. Uncover, fluff the rice with a fork, and stir in the reserved onions. Adjust seasoning if necessary and remove the bay leaf and thyme.

Serve jollof rice while still warm with a side of Dòdò (page 193) and Braised Goat Leg in Ọbẹ (page 223).

A toasted corn snack, àádùn in Yorùbá can be translated as, "It is going to be good." With àádùn, a little goes a long way: a handful of these is all you need to experience their delicate oily crunch and dry-roasted nut aroma. Finely ground cornmeal works best, and red palm oil holds it all together.

Àádùn

SERVES 8 TO 10

3 cups roasted cornmeal (page 254)

½ teaspoon fine salt

½ teaspoon cayenne pepper

½ cup to ¾ cup red palm oil

8 frozen banana leaves, thawed and cut into 10-inch squares

Twine or string for wrapping

In a medium bowl, combine the cornmeal, salt, and cayenne pepper and whisk to incorporate. Pour in the palm oil and knead with your hands until the mixture begins to come together and forms a dough when pressed together. Once it comes together, you have enough oil in there.

Serve àádùn in a bowl with banana leaves on the side so each guest can take a portion and make little packages using the leaves and twine. Alternatively wrap individual portions to hand out to guests. Àádùn is made for sharing!

NOTE Àádùn can be part of any ceremony marking beginnings—naming ceremonies, new engagements, weddings, or family occasions—and is perfect for sharing, symbolizing the hope for a sweet life. I've often seen it divided into small portions and wrapped in a banana leaf, then handed to attending guests to carry with them.

Àádùn can now be found sold streetside at major transit hubs and especially along the Lagos-Ibadan Expressway. It is said to have originated in Abeokuta by the Egbas, who are often considered to be the best àádùn makers.

My grandmother loved her àkàrà pressed flat while frying to ensure crunchy edges. She wanted a crisp texture in every bite. My favorite memory of àkàrà is receiving courier packages from her to our home in Ikeja. The àkàrà, wrapped in oil-soaked paper packages, arrived promptly to mark an event: a birth in the family, a move to a new home, a safe return from travel, or sometimes to honor the memory of a deceased relative.

Traditionally, àkàrà is a celebration food. The plump rounds should be cake-like and fluffy on the inside with a golden exterior. Popular in Yorùbá cuisine, it's a simple dish that requires a careful hand when prepared. Each step from pureeing the ingredients, mixing the batter, and frying is critical to developing layers of flavor and texture.

Àkàrà is best served warm as a meal when paired with Ògi (page 42), as a small chop enjoyed by itself, or as a sandwich filling between pillowy-soft agége bread slices.

Àkàrà

YIELD: 6 TO 8 SERVINGS (32 PIECES)

2 cups èwà olóyin or black eyed peas, soaked and peeled, or 1½ cups bean powder

¼ cup finely diced yellow onion

2 garlic cloves

1 Scotch bonnet pepper, stemmed

1¼ teaspoons fine salt, plus more to taste

4 cups peanut oil or red palm oil

Working in batches, transfer the peeled beans to a food processor and puree with up to 1 cup water until smooth. Stir in the diced onion, garlic, and Scotch bonnet pepper. Add the 1¼ teaspoons salt and puree to the consistency of slightly coarse whipped hummus. If using bean powder, skip the puree and salt step and just stir in ½ cup water. The batter should be thick enough to hold its shape softly.

Heat the peanut oil to 350°F. Working in batches to avoid crowding, use a spoon to transfer tablespoon-size portions to the hot oil. Fry until cooked through and golden brown, turning frequently to cook evenly on all sides, about 6 minutes. Remove from the oil and drain on a cooling rack inserted in a baking sheet or on a plate lined with paper towels. Repeat the frying process for the remaining batter until it is used up.

Serve the àkàrà while still warm, alone or along with a warm bowl of Èko (page 117), or as a sandwich between slices of Agége (page 115).

While the stew itself may be more accurately described as a caramelized relish, especially the versions common to Lagos, it's called Ofada stew because it has traditionally been served with a fragrant heirloom rice from the Ofada region of southwestern Nigeria.

Ofada stew can be found on menus across Lagos, everywhere from music venues to cafeterias to bukas. Its rich, decadent flavors are powerful enough to linger on your palate and its aromatic ingredients create a fragrance that seems to seep into the very clothes you're wearing. I am practically addicted to the many variations I find whenever I'm in Lagos. If it's on the menu, I'm ordering it.

Ofada is made with palm oil, crayfish, and lots of irú—the very fragrant anchors of our cuisine's complexity. Different cuts of meats can be stirred in depending on your preferences, and red or green peppers work equally well as the base for the sauce.

Ofada Stew

YIELD: 2 CUPS

½ cup red palm oil

1 small red onion, peeled and minced

2 to 3 tablespoons Trinity Pepper Paste (page 102)

¼ cup irú

4 cups Ata Gígé (page 89)

Fine salt to taste

1 pound assorted cooked meats or roast mushrooms (see page 166), optional

Steamed rice and Dòdò (page 193), for serving

In a large shallow saucepan, heat up the palm oil over medium heat and add in the onions. Saute the onions until softened and just beginning to brown, about 8 minutes. Add the pepper paste and stir till fragrant, about 1 minute. Pour in the irú and ata gígé and bring up to a simmer. Reduce heat to medium, cover, and let simmer until the sauce is thickened and reduced to about half of its original volume, about 20 minutes.

Season sauce with salt to taste. Add in any cooked meats or mushrooms, if using, stir to coat in sauce and cook until warmed through, about 6 minutes. Serve immediately with steamed rice and dòdò.

This is a personal favorite of mine when eating out in Lagos, especially when it's served with periwinkles, which is a seafood that feels luxurious because it can be difficult to source. I've opted for blue crabs here, which feel just as indulgent. Finished with red palm oil, the soup is nourishing and elegant. A starchy swallow (page 52) should be included to complement it.

This soup is a delicacy from the southeastern regions of Nigeria and well known among the Efik in Calabar. Afang leaves are rich in protein, folic acid, and vitamin A, and are especially good for women who are pregnant or nursing. Dried afang leaves are available in African grocery stores across the diaspora.

Afang Soup WITH BLUE CRABS

SERVES 4

2 cups rehydrated or frozen afang leaves or 4 cups fresh leaves

4 tablespoons red palm oil

1 medium onion, chopped

1 to 2 tablespoons Trinity Pepper Paste (page 102)

½ cup large dried crayfish, soaked in hot water

2 cups fish stock (page 80) or vegetable stock

1 pound fresh blue crabs, cleaned

4 cups chopped gbúre or mature spinach leaves (optional)

Fine salt to taste

Òkèlè (page 52), for serving

Chop the rehydrated afang leaves with ½ cup water in a blender or food processor.

In a medium-size Dutch oven, heat 2 tablespoons of the palm oil over medium heat. Add the onion and sauté until just softened, about 3 minutes. Add the pepper paste and cook until fragrant, about 1 minute. Stir in the dried crayfish, stock, and crabs. Bring the liquid to a simmer and allow the crabs to steam in the broth until they just turn bright red, about 8 minutes.

Reduce the heat and stir in the gbúre or spinach leaves, if using. Add the chopped afang leaves. Fold in and allow to cook for 5 to 6 minutes. Stir in the remaining 2 tablespoons palm oil, taste and adjust seasoning with salt, and cook until soup is warmed through, about 5 minutes.

Serve the afang soup warm with òkèlè, such as èbà (see headnote, page 49), pounded yam, or any steamed starch, such as plantains, yam, potatoes, or cassava.

This is often the centerpiece of my dinners, and something I love to build toward. Starting with snacks and small chops, then shifting to elegantly composed soups and stews is essentially my fine dining take on the comfort foods I've loved my whole life. This dish is part of the main entrée, served family style and centered on a wide platter: a bone-in leg of goat coated in caramelized red sauce and piled high with freshly scissored herbs. The flavors are bold, fiery, and peppery, and more than any other dish it is my conversation starter.

If cooked in the pot with the sauce, this goat leg will attain a fall-off-the-bone tenderness. You will encounter this in restaurants in Lagos and in bukas across the world, usually butchered into almost bite-sized pieces with the skin, bones, and cartilage visible. However you serve it, make sure it is accompanied by steamed rice, jollof rice, fried sweet plantains, or crispy yam fries.

Braised Goat Leg in Ọbẹ̀

SERVES 8 TO 10

- 2 tablespoons grapeseed oil
- One 4- to 5-pound bone-in goat leg
- Kosher salt
- 1 garlic bulb, cut crosswise
- 3 large carrots, tops trimmed, cut into 2-inch pieces
- 2 large onions, chopped
- One 14.5-ounce can whole peeled tomatoes
- 10 fresh thyme sprigs
- 2 fresh bay leaves

- 1 red habanero chile
- 4 cups beef or chicken stock (page 79)
- 4 cups Ata Lílọ̀ (page 90)
- 1 lemon, zested into strips, then julienned lengthwise
- ¼ cup cilantro leaves and tender stems
- ¼ cup parsley leaves and tender stems
- ¼ cup sliced green onions or scallions

Heat oil in a large Dutch oven or heavy-bottomed pot over medium-high. Season the goat leg generously on all sides with salt, then sear, turning frequently, until brown, 16 to 18 minutes. Transfer the leg to a large plate using tongs.

Preheat the oven to 350°F. Sear the garlic, cut side down, in the rendered fat until golden brown, about 2 minutes. Transfer to the plate. Add the carrots and onions to the pot and cook until browned around the edges, about 8 minutes. Add the tomatoes and their juices, tearing apart the whole pieces into large chunks as you add them. Stir in the thyme, bay leaves, and habanero.

Add the stock and bring the sauce to a simmer over medium-high heat. Return

continued >

Braised Goat Leg in Ọbẹ̀

< continued

the goat and garlic to the pot, cover, and transfer to the oven. Braise until the meat is just tender but not falling apart, about 3 hours.

Remove the pot from the oven and increase the oven temperature to 375°F. Transfer the goat to a large plate using tongs. Add the ata lílọ̀ to the pot and bring the sauce up to a simmer over medium high. Cook, stirring occasionally, until the flavors of the broth and ata have come together and the sauce has thickened slightly, about 20 minutes. Season with salt and place the goat leg back in, ladling the sauce over the top of the goat if it is not completely submerged. Cover with the lid and return it to the oven. Braise until the goat is tender enough to pull with a fork and just beginning to fall off the bone, about 45 minutes.

The best way to serve this is warm, dinner-party style, right from the pot or on a large platter for guests to share. Scatter the top with the lemon zest, cilantro, parsley, and green onions. Serve with steamed plain rice or jollof rice, dòdò, and a side of èfọ́ rírò.

When I worked at my friend Olamidé's Nigerian restaurant Peju's Kitchen in Baltimore, Maryland, I noticed that the regulars expected us to have móín móín on the weekends. It reminded me that growing up we too ate this on weekends, because of the amount of time invested with each step in the process. It's hardly time-consuming with practice, but it was only while working closely with Olamidé that I learned the precise techniques for móín móín that I'm sharing here.

Móín móín is a pureed bean paste wrapped and steamed in òle leaves. Òle is a variety of water lily leaf, but I've adapted this recipe for banana leaves, which work just as well. Folded pieces of foil or parchment, ramekins, small bowls, or even corn husks can be used to hold and steam the wonderfully fragrant bean paste.

The trick to this dish is finding the right consistency, and so many factors—from humidity to ingredient moisture to texture—affect its outcome. If the batter has too little water, the móín móín will come out as dense lumps. If the consistency is too loose, they won't form at all. Perfecting móín móín goes beyond the batter itself—there's a fluffiness to the finished product, and an almost cake-like consistency that you're

continued >

looking to achieve. With this texture comes a bouquet of aromas and a rich, luxurious mouthfeel.

Good mọ́ín mọ́ín reveals layers of flavors that build as you eat. What begins as a creamy richness soon builds to a slightly smoky, spicy, dense hardiness—a sensory combination that few other dishes can produce. In this way, mọ́ín mọ́ín stays on the palate, its complex depth of flavor lingering long after the last bite is gone. It's a true reward for the time invested.

Mọ́ín Mọ́ín

SERVES 6

2 cups ẹ̀wà olóyin, soaked and peeled, or 1½ cups bean powder

1 red bell pepper, stemmed and seeded

1 small yellow onion, diced

1 red Scotch bonnet pepper, stemmed

2 teaspoons salt, plus more to taste

½ cup melted Manshanu (page 96), lard, or grapeseed oil

¼ cup red palm oil

2 tablespoons whole dried crayfish, soaked in hot water to rehydrate

Fine salt to taste

2 frozen packs banana leaves, defrosted, for steaming

1 cup smoked catfish fillet, cleaned and bones removed, for garnish

2 soft-boiled eggs, peeled and quartered, for garnish

Ata Dín Dín (page 93), for dipping

Working in batches, transfer the peeled beans to a food processor and puree with up to 1 cup water until smooth. Add the bell pepper, diced onion, and Scotch bonnet pepper. Season with 2 teaspoons salt and puree to the consistency of whipped hummus. The batter should softly hold its shape. Transfer to a medium bowl and stir in the melted manshanu, palm oil, and soaked crayfish.

Line a wide shallow pot with leaves. Pour about 2 cups of water behind the leaves into the bottom of the pot and bring to a gentle simmer over low heat.

Fold a banana leaf into a cone. Hold a corner down toward you on your work surface so the edges are pointing down in a V-shape. Grab an edge and move in toward the center. The straight edge should line up with the center of the leaf. Hold the edge down and with your other hand, grab the second edge in over and around the first fold. Lift up the folded leaf and tuck the bottom point upward to seal. Line any tears on the inside of the cone with little pieces of leaves to seal further. Hold the cone in an upright position, keeping the bottom edge sealed by pinching together, ladle in some of the batter, just enough to fill about halfway. Add in a few pieces of smoked catfish and a quarter piece of soft-boiled eggs.

Fold the top of the cone over itself and tuck the seam behind the leaf. Place the filled cone seam side down in the pot. Repeat this process until all the batter and leaves are used up, placing the filled cones beside each other in the pot. Place several more leaves over the top and cover the pot with a lid. Steam the mọ́ín mọ́ín until firm, about 20 minutes.

Serve warm or room temperature alongside èkọ or èkọ tutu for breakfast, or with any of the rice dishes with some ata dín dín for dipping.

This is an all-purpose rice recipe that feels central to the way we Nigerians entertain. It is milder than jollof rice, making it an ideal option for hosts of big celebrations who want something that pleases everyone. The rice is not meant to be the star, but it can be accented with spices and herbs in a variety of ways.

This version features a toasted peppersoup spice blend that I often add to my fried rice at home. Since many of the starches central to Nigerian cuisine—plantain, yam, and millet to name a few—have distinctive flavor profiles on their own, this dish always serves as the relatively simple base for variations depending on the seasons. In this version, I incorporate crispy shallots, Calabash nutmeg, and whichever fresh herbs are in the garden—scent leaf, cilantro, or parsley. There's room for fresh lemongrass as well if you have it handy.

Fried Rice
WITH CRISPY SHALLOTS AND HERBS

SERVES 4

¼ cup grapeseed oil

4 shallots, thinly sliced

Fine salt to taste

2 tablespoons Manshanu (page 96)

2-inch piece of ginger, peeled and grated

2 garlic cloves, grated

1 tender stalk of lemongrass, finely chopped (optional)

2 teaspoons ground turmeric

2 tablespoons Toasted Peppersoup Spice (page 99)

4 cups cooked short-grain rice, cooled to room temperature

¼ cup sliced green onions or scallions

2 tablespoons julienned scent leaf

¼ cup fresh cilantro leaves

In a large pot or Dutch oven, heat the oil over medium heat until shimmering, 1 to 2 minutes. Add the shallots and cook, stirring frequently until golden brown, 5 to 8 minutes. Remove the shallots from the oil and allow to drain on paper towels or a cooling rack. Season with salt and set aside. Drain all but 2 tablespoons of the cooking oil out of the pot (save the drained shallot-flavored oil for another use).

Add the manshanu and gently melt over medium heat. Add the ginger, garlic, lemongrass, if using, and turmeric. Sauté until fragrant, about 2 minutes. Add the peppersoup spice and rice and toss to combine. Cook, stirring frequently until the rice is warmed through and fragrant, 3 to 4 minutes. Remove from the heat and transfer to a platter.

Top the rice with the crispy shallots, green onions, scent leaf, and cilantro. Serve immediately.

Sunday was chicken day at our family's house in Ikeja, Lagos, and the result was a dinner sourced almost entirely from the backyard: freshly picked herbs to elevate the senses, ripe citrus to add acid to the drippings, seasoning blends my mother made and stored in her pantry, and of course, the chicken itself (several of which we kept year-round in a broad enclosure). There's no buka in Lagos that serves a dish quite like this, but the flavor components are recognizable. And coconut rice, of course, can be found across Lagos.

This is something that has become a Sunday tradition for me and my family in Brooklyn. Even the herb seasoning arrives with my mother on her visits (see page 97), and it gives me an enormous sense of joy to share it with you. Serve this with any of the condiments and sauces from the previous chapters.

Mom's Sunday Chicken
WITH COCONUT RICE

SERVES 4

1 whole 3½- to 4-pound chicken or 2 Cornish hens

¼ cup Manshanu (page 96)

1 shallot, minced

1-inch piece of ginger, peeled and grated

1 tablespoon Omotunde's Spice Blend (page 97)

1 tablespoon salt, plus more to taste

2 medium onions, quartered lengthwise

1 stalk of lemongrass, cut into 3- to 4-inch pieces and smashed with the back of a knife

1 garlic bulb, cut crosswise

2 cups long-grain rice such as jasmine or basmati

1 cup full-fat coconut milk

1 tablespoon lime zest

2 green onions, roots trimmed, thinly sliced

¼ cup large unsweetened coconut flakes, toasted

Preheat the oven to 375°F.

Pat the chicken dry with paper towels. Using your fingers, gently lift the skin around the chicken breast and thighs up from the flesh.

In a small bowl, combine the manshanu, shallot, ginger, and the spice blend. Use a fork to combine into a smooth paste.

Without tearing the skin, gently spread tablespoonfuls of the compound man-shanu underneath the skin. Rub whatever is left of the manshanu around the chicken cavity. Season the inside and outside with 1 tablespoon salt. Truss the chicken by tying the legs together with kitchen twine and tucking in the wing tips.

continued >

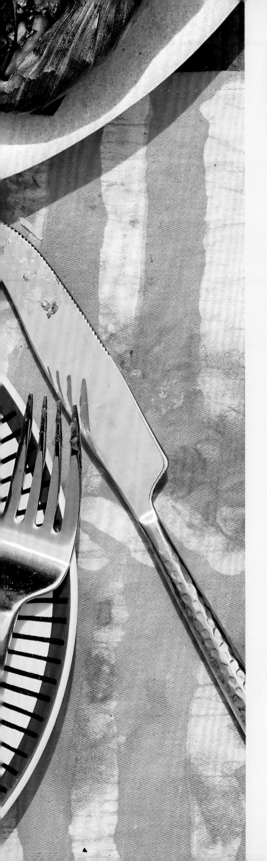

Mom's Sunday Chicken with Coconut Rice

< continued

In a large 8-quart clay pot or Dutch oven, layer the onions, lemongrass, and garlic in the bottom of the pot. Place the chicken on top of the vegetables. Cover and roast in the oven for 40 minutes.

While the chicken is roasting, prepare the coconut rice. In a small pot, combine the rice with 2 cups of water and the coconut milk. Season with salt and bring to a simmer over medium heat. Cook until the rice is just tender, 12 to 15 minutes. Allow the cooked rice to sit covered until you are ready to serve.

Increase the oven temperature to 400°F, uncover the chicken, and continue to roast for an additional 25 to 30 minutes, until the chicken is golden and the meat quite tender. The juices should run clear and an oven thermometer inserted in the thickest part of the thigh should be at least 165°F.

Remove from the oven, transfer the chicken to a board, and allow to rest for at least 15 minutes before serving.

Just before serving, add the lime zest, sliced green onions, and toasted coconut flakes to the rice. Fluff with a fork and sprinkle some more spice blend over the top.

Carve the chicken and serve topped with the onions tossed in the pan drippings, coconut rice, dòdò (fried sweet plantains), and any or all of the following condiment sauces: Ata Dín Dín (page 93), Ofada Stew (page 220), and Trinity Pepper Paste (page 102).

Lagos's many inland harbors and lagoons allow for exceptional fishing, and this stew captures the essence of the coast's influence in our cuisine and ingredients. You'll find similar seafood-based stews throughout West Africa and in the diaspora.

The stew is peppery and bright, with a brothy tomato base laced with Scotch bonnets. The seafood is poached until it reaches a soft tenderness. Handfuls of scent leaf and cilantro sharpen the broth, complementing the tender seafood.

Because its brothy consistency balances well when combined with thicker soups, this stew can be served with draw soups like Ilá (grated okra, page 161) and Ewédú (page 162).

Fisherman's Stew

SERVES 8

2 tablespoons red palm oil

1 small red onion, chopped

4 garlic cloves, sliced

2 tablespoons tomato paste

4 cups Ata Lílọ̀ (page 90)

3 cups fish stock (page 80) or vegetable stock

2 to 3 fresh crabs, cleaned and halved

1 pound bone-in catfish, grouper, mackerel, or snapper steaks

½ pound large head-on prawns, deveined

¼ cup cilantro leaves and tender stems

¼ cup chopped dill leaves and tender stems

¼ cup scent leaf

Steamed rice or swallow (page 52), for serving

In a large pot, heat up the oil over medium-high heat. Add in the onions and sauté until softened and translucent, about 5 minutes. Add the garlic and sauté until just fragrant, about 1 minute. Add in the tomato paste and cook until darkened. Stir in the ata lílọ̀ and stock. Bring the pot up to a boil and allow to simmer until just slightly reduced, about 12 to 15 minutes.

Gently add in the crabs and allow them to simmer for 4 to 5 minutes until their color changes to a bright orange. Add in the fish and cook until flesh is just beginning to flake, 2 to 3 minutes. Stir in prawns, and simmer for additional 2 minutes (or until the prawns are cooked through).

Combine the cilantro, dill and scent leaf in a small bowl and use to garnish the stew while still in the pot. Serve fisherman's stew over rice, or alongside Ilá (page 161) or Ewédú (page 162) and any of the Òkèlè on page 52.

Although this recipe hails from northern Nigeria, the use of spiced or roasted groundnut in soups is typical in West African cooking. My father would return from business trips in the north with stories of quiet meals surrounded by new acquaintances, and dishes such as these were meant to serve as something more than sustenance. Miyan taushe, with ingredients recognizable to all Nigerians and West Africans in general, is a unifying and comforting dish that allows people of different cultures and backgrounds to find familiar culinary ground.

Peanuts feature heavily in the cuisine of the north. Miyan taushe holds up well among starches and stews alike. You can pair this with a lighter, brighter side dish, or with something that communicates the heat of a Scotch bonnet. The most typical accompanying starches are rice, Tuwo (page 56), Sinasir (page 204), and Funkaso (page 200).

Miyan Taushe

YIELD: 4 CUPS

2 tablespoons peanut oil

1 red onion, diced

4 garlic cloves, minced

1 tablespoon dawadawa powder

1 tablespoon tomato paste

One 14.5-ounce can whole peeled tomatoes

1 small pumpkin (about 2 pounds), peeled, and cut into pieces

1 red Scotch bonnet, poked all around with the tip of a knife

3 cups vegetable stock or water

1 cup Gyada Paste (page 46) or ½ cup unsalted natural peanut butter

2 tablespoons red palm oil

4 cups baby spinach leaves

Fine salt to taste

In a large saucepan, heat the oil over medium heat and add the onion. Sauté until soft and golden but not browned, about 3 minutes. Add the garlic and dawadawa powder and stir until fragrant, about 30 seconds. Add the tomato paste and cook until the color deepens to a dark red, about 3 minutes.

Add the peeled tomatoes with their liquid. Crush the tomatoes with your hands as they go in. Stir and scrape the bottom of the pan to loosen any bits. Allow the sauce to come to a simmer. Add the pumpkin pieces and the Scotch bonnet pepper. Stir in the stock and bring to a simmer. Cook the sauce until the pumpkin is tender but not falling apart, about 15 minutes.

Add the gyada paste or peanut butter, and cook until the sauce thickens, stirring frequently. Using your wooden spoon, crush pieces of the pumpkin into the sauce to give it body. Pour in the palm oil and cook another few minutes. Before serving, stir in the spinach leaves and season to taste with salt.

Also known as "white soup," this dish may seem like a straightforward combination of basic ingredients, but upon first taste you'll discover a complex layering of flavors. Steamed, mashed, and pureed yams are its smooth and silky base. While an attention to detail and careful monitoring of the yam's texture as it is incorporated into the sauce make this dish best suited for home kitchens, you may encounter ofe nsala at restaurants in Lagos for a hefty price.

One of the rare Nigerian soups where red bell peppers or palm oil are absent from the base, it hails from the eastern and southeastern regions of Nigeria, especially Anambra State.

Ofe Nsala
WITH LARGE PRAWNS

SERVES 4

1 large yam

Fine salt to taste

15 to 20 large prawns, heads and tails on

4 cups meat or chicken stock (page 79) or vegetable stock

1 tablespoon Trinity Pepper Paste (page 102)

2 dried catfish, cleaned and rinsed

¼ cup rehydrated dried afang leaves

4 cups sliced fresh greens such as mature spinach (optional)

Remove the brown skin on the yam by peeling off with a paring knife or a vegetable peeler. Slice the peeled yam into pieces and keep in a bowl of water to keep from oxidizing. Rinse off the yam pieces and place in a medium saucepan. Cover with water and bring to a boil over medium-high heat. Season with salt and reduce the heat to a simmer. Allow the yam to cook until completely softened, 10 to 12 minutes.

While the yams are cooking, use a sharp knife or large kitchen shears to cut open along the length of the back of each prawn. Cut deep enough to expose and remove the vein running down the prawn.

Drain off any remaining liquid from the yam and once cooled enough to handle, crush the yam into smaller pieces using your fingers or the back of a fork. Cover and set aside.

Bring the stock up to a simmer in a large pot set over medium-high heat. Gently poach the cleaned prawns by dropping them into the simmering broth. Cook until the prawns turn pink and firm, 1 to 2 minutes. Move the prawns to a plate and set aside.

Into the broth, stir in the pepper paste, dried catfish, and afang leaves. Allow to simmer until the liquid is reduced to about three-quarters of the original volume. Strain the stock through a fine-mesh sieve to remove and discard the solids.

Using a blender, carefully puree 2 cups of the stock mixture with the crushed yam pieces until smooth. Return the mixture to the pot, along with the remaining stock. Using a wooden spoon, stir the soup while cooking over low heat. Stir in the poached shrimp and adjust the seasoning with more salt if necessary. Add any fresh greens, if using. Cook until warmed through and beginning to simmer, 4 to 5 minutes. Divide the soup and prawns among bowls and serve warm.

Ẹ̀fọ́ is the word the Yorùbá use to describe fresh leafy greens. Ẹ̀fọ́ rírò is stewed greens—the ultimate comfort food. I make mine smoky and spicy in a base of ata dín dín with large flakes of smoked mackerel. The greens balance the robust flavors that build in your pot. If you have an overflow of greens from a market trip or a backyard harvest, then it's the perfect time to make ẹ̀fọ́ rírò.

Ẹ̀fọ́ tẹ́tẹ́ or Amaranth greens, also known as callaloo in the Caribbean, is still my go-to green when I can get my hands on a fresh bunch. Other greens such as mature spinach or collards, fresh or frozen, make an adequate substitute. Typically served alongside pounded yam and a bowl of assorted meats, ẹ̀fọ́ rírò is also a nice complement to any rice dish.

Ẹ̀fọ́ Rírò
WITH SMOKED MACKEREL

YIELD: 6 TO 8 SERVINGS (ABOUT 7 CUPS)

3 pounds fresh amaranth greens (also known as tẹ́tẹ́ or callaloo) or mature spinach, or 2 pounds frozen whole-leaf spinach, thawed

2 tablespoons red palm oil

1 medium onion, peeled and minced

2 tablespoons Trinity Pepper Paste (page 102)

2 cups Ofada Stew (page 220)

Fine salt

1½ cups flaked smoked mackerel or smoked white fish, skin and bones removed (from about three 3 ounce fillets)

If using fresh greens, bring a large pot of salted water up to a boil over medium-high heat and set up an ice bath in a large bowl. Pick the leaves off the bunch of greens and discard the tough stems. Once the water is boiling, working in batches, blanch the leaves until bright green and just tender, about 2 minutes. Cool the greens immediately in the ice bath. Skip this blanching step if using frozen spinach.

In a large skillet, heat the oil over medium-high heat and sauté the onion until softened, about 6 minutes. Add in the pepper paste. Sauté until fragrant, about 1 minute.

Pour in the Ofada stew, stir, and bring up to a simmer. Reduce the heat to medium simmer until sauce thickens slightly, 8 to 10 minutes.

Season with salt and cook for an additional minute.

Remove the greens from the ice bath and squeeze out as much water as possible so you don't dilute the vibrant flavors of the sauce. If using frozen greens, defrost a day ahead and squeeze out any excess liquid before using.

Add the greens to the skillet and stir to coat with the sauce. Add the smoked fish pieces and gently stir to distribute into the greens. Cook further to just warm up the greens and fish, 4 to 5 minutes. Season to taste and remove from the heat.

Ẹ̀fọ́ rírò is served as an accompaniment to any starch staples, or enjoy over a bowl of steamed rice and a side of Dòdò (page 193).

SWEETS

Classic Nigerian cuisine does not have the kind of relationship to the dessert course as I've experienced living abroad. Dessert does not share equal billing on a menu, and there are no award shows or bake offs that heighten Nigerian confections to a competitive art. What we have can be classified as "sweets," drawing from both pre- and post-colonial ideas of what role a sweet should play in the meal.

There is certainly a category of foods in Nigerian cuisine that are sweet, but dessert as a course depends upon the country's tropical seasons, and starts with freshly picked fruit placed in a bowl. When I host dinners, I lean into my past as a pastry cook and apply those experiences to Nigerian cuisine. The recipes in this chapter offer a selection of snacks and fruit-heavy courses with a few of my childhood favorites.

My mother was a food scientist and worked at the Cadbury branch in Nigeria throughout my childhood, so we were never without new recipes or bits and pieces of whatever she was working on. We also had access to stabilizers and sweeteners that made making candy at home easier than it should have been in a hot, humid city like Lagos. For a child, there are never enough sweets at home, so I would sneak bites after school from any vendor that was strategically planted just outside the schoolyard.

Sweets are encountered like this all throughout Lagos, especially in crowded markets where vendors specialize in the kinds of snacks that can be eaten quickly on-the-go. But sweets are treated informally even in formal settings. After-dinner bites will center on sugar or fruit, and occasionally both at once. It is this clash of the pre- and post-colonial that makes our sweets so unique.

I have friends who swear they don't eat dessert but will devour a small bowl of freshly picked star fruit, pureed mango, or neatly cut caramels dusted in coconut. The freshness of our fruits make our sweets so irresistible, and is central to the way our cuisine has maintained its connection to the natural world—even in a fast-paced megacity.

These take me back to my childhood, when candy vendors would congregate just beyond the front gates of my school in Lagos. Chocolate brown in color (they're called bàbá dúdú in Yorùbá, which refers to their brown hue) and wrapped in plastic, these confections hung from the vendors' stalls like little jewels. Just one was a sweet reward to myself for enduring another day at school, a treat I finished quickly before I was picked up. While recipe testing, I found that they are quite versatile and great as either a soft, chewy morsel or as a rich, flavorful hard candy. Store either version in an airtight container for up to two weeks.

Coconut Milk Caramels

YIELD: 12 TO 16 CARAMELS

Coconut oil or cooking spray

One 13.5-ounce can unsweetened coconut cream (or one 13.5-ounce can unsweetened coconut milk)

2 cups sugar

2 tablespoons honey

½ teaspoon fine sea salt

1 cup unsweetened coconut flakes, toasted

Line an 8-inch baking pan with parchment and brush with coconut oil or coat with cooking spray.

In a medium-size heavy-bottom saucepan, combine the coconut cream or milk, sugar, honey, and sea salt. Cook the mixture over medium heat, stirring frequently until it reaches 300° to 350°F on a candy thermometer, 25 to 35 minutes. Pour the caramel into the prepared pan and allow to cool completely.

Once cool, spread an even layer of toasted coconut over the top of the caramel. Invert onto a board or clean surface. Peel off the layer of parchment and scatter more coconut flakes over the top. If you want even-size squares, slice the caramel while still warm. Once the caramel is completely cool, break into pieces.

You can wrap these as individual sweets using parchment, wax paper, or cellophane wrappers and twist the ends to seal. Store in an airtight container at room temperature in a cool dry place for up to 2 weeks.

Kunu gyada is a creamy porridge of crushed rice cooked in fresh groundnut milk. Because it's filling yet easily digestible, I found it to be helpful when I was weaning my daughters. Short-grain rice imparts a subtle sweetness to this creamy, peanutty blend. Aromatic cinnamon, nutmeg, ginger and cloves—or any other warming spices—meld into the comforting porridge, which is often served at the beginning or end of the day in northern Nigeria to fill the gap between meals.

Aṣa loves a warm bowl of kunu gyada with just a little honey stirred in, but a dab of tamarind paste, crushed peanuts, and even a spoon of fruit compote or fresh fruit all make fine toppings.

Kunu Gyada
(Rice and Groundnut Porridge)

SERVES 6

2 cups shelled and skinned raw peanuts

½ cup short-grain white rice, such as sushi rice

1 tablespoon Toasted Spice Blend (page 101)

Tamarind Paste (page 98) and granulated sugar, honey, or chopped dates, for serving

Place the raw peanuts and rice in separate bowls, and add enough water to cover each by 2 inches. Soak at room temperature for at least 1 hour and up to 4 hours.

continued >

Kunu Gyada

< continued

Drain the peanuts and transfer to a blender. Pour in 2 cups room-temperature water and puree on high speed until smooth. Strain the liquid through a fine-mesh strainer or a sieve lined with muslin or two layers of cheesecloth, into a medium pot. Return the solids to the blender and combine with another 2 cups room-temperature water. Blend on high until pureed. Repeat the straining process, pressing on the solids to extract as much liquid as possible. The remaining solids should be dry and crumbly. Discard the solids. You should have 4 cups of peanut milk in the pot.

Drain the rice and transfer to the blender (no need to wash). Pour in 2 cups room-temperature water and puree on high to grind the rice until smooth.

To the pot of peanut milk, add the sweet spice blend. Heat the milk and spices over medium, whisking frequently, until steam begins to rise from the surface, about 6 minutes.

Turn the heat to medium-low and whisk in the ground rice puree. Cook, stirring frequently until the mixture is thick enough for your whisk to leave a faint line as you drag it across the surface and any bubbles slowly rise to the surface, 8 minutes. Cover and simmer without stirring for about 4 minutes to fully cook the ground rice. Any coarse ground rice should be cooked through and soft, not starchy.

Serve the porridge in bowls warm or at room temperature. Top with a spoonful of tamarind paste for a slightly tangy finish and sweeten with granulated sugar, honey, or chopped dates.

My mom's friend Alhaja Lawal ran the staff canteen at Cadbury's Lagos office. She embodied the quintessential host, and she made the world's best chin chin: thin, crispy, mildly sweet, and absolutely irresistible. My brothers and I could count on a bag or two of it on the occasional after-school stop at mum's office. After I moved to the United States, mum would pack a suitcase full of nostalgic childhood snacks, including sealed bags of Alhaja's chin chin.

A good batch of chin chin should carry a hint of seasoning and as little flavor from the oil as possible. The dough can be rolled out thick or thin, depending on how crisp you prefer them. I prefer the thinner version that fries up golden brown and crispy. Small plates of chin chin are brilliant little welcome snacks—a plate of ipanu (easy-to-grab bites): nothing to fuss over, but something to keep your tastebuds busy.

Chin Chin

SERVES 8 TO 10

2¾ cups all-purpose flour, plus more for dusting

½ cup sugar

½ teaspoon fine sea salt

¼ teaspoon nutmeg

¼ cup (2 ounces) chilled butter

2 large yolks, lightly beaten

About 4 cups vegetable oil, for frying

In a large bowl, combine the flour, sugar, sea salt, and nutmeg. Add the butter and cut into the flour mixture until it resembles coarse bread crumbs. Make a well in the center and add the egg yolks and ½ cup water. Incorporate the ingredients until the mixture resembles a shaggy dough. Pour the dough out onto a very lightly floured surface and press together to form a smooth dough. Wrap with plastic and chill for at least an hour before rolling out. At this point the dough will keep for up to 1 week in the refrigerator or for up to a month in the freezer.

Lightly dust a work surface with flour and cut the dough in half. Starting with one half, roll out the dough into a thin sheet (¼ to ½ inch thick). Cut

the dough into ¼-inch-wide strips, then again into ¼-inch-wide squares. Dust the squares lightly with flour, move to a baking sheet, and roll out the remaining dough.

Heat about 4 cups of vegetable oil in a medium saucepan over medium heat to about 325°F. Working in batches, fry the dough squares until crisp and golden brown, 5 to 6 minutes per batch. Use a slotted spoon to move the chin chin to a plate lined with paper towels or a cooling rack inserted in a baking sheet to drain. Serve the chin chin completely cooled in bowls or plates, for sharing.

Once cool, chin chin will keep stored in an airtight container for up to a week.

Chuk chuk is one of the few recipes I learned by watching my Oma George. This was a snack she would make with fresh coconut by grating the flesh and pressing out the milk. What remained would be semi-dry bits of coconut flesh, the base for this confection of coconut clusters encased in a dry caramel.

While I do miss the fresh coconut taste of these candies, I'm not pressing the milk out of coconut pieces here in my Brooklyn kitchen. Luckily, large unsweetened coconut flakes do the trick for me. My ratio of coconut flakes to caramel ensures a light, crispy confection. As is the case with most of my confections, I add a little salt for balance. Great for snacking, ending a meal, or wrapping in little bags as gifts, chuk chuk is an easy and delightful treat to make. I store at room temperature in an airtight container, usually a glass jar with a lid, where it'll keep for up to one week.

Chuk Chuk (aka Shuk Shuk)

YIELD: 1 DOZEN

2 cups
unsweetened large
flake coconut

½ cup granulated
sugar

2 tablespoons
honey

½ teaspoon
sea salt

Spread the coconut flakes out on a baking sheet and allow to dry while you make the caramel. You can do this process at least a day ahead of time.

In a medium saucepan, combine the sugar, honey, and salt and stir to incorporate with a spatula. Over medium-high heat, cook the sugar until the grains dissolve into a syrup. Cook the syrup until golden and lightly caramelized. Stir in the coconut flakes at this point and remove from the heat.

Drop tablespoon-size portions of the coconut candy on a lightly oiled baking sheet and allow to cool completely. Store the candy in an airtight container at room temperature for up to a week.

Sisí pẹlẹbẹ is the Yorùbá name for this brittle of ground peanuts poured into salted caramel. It can be found in a variety of flavors, shapes, and sizes across West Africa. I use my gyada paste here for convenience, but crushed peanuts work just as well. Whole benne seeds can also work well. As with any ingredient that gets immersed in a pot of warm caramel, the nuts end up lightly toasted and fragrant. In Lagos, they are cut into signature diamond and hexagonal shapes while the caramel is still warm and not completely set. Here, I allow the confection to cool and set completely on its baking sheet before cracking it into smaller pieces. Store in an airtight container at room temperature for up to a week.

Sisí Pẹlẹbẹ

SERVES 8 TO 10

2 cups sugar

1 cup honey

½ teaspoon fine salt

1 cup raw, no-skin peanuts, roughly chopped, plus more for sprinkling

2 teaspoons baking soda

Prepare a baking sheet by brushing with melted butter (include the sides).

In a medium-size pot, over high heat, combine the sugar, honey, salt, and 1 cup water. Stir frequently until the mixture comes to a boil. Reduce the heat to medium and allow it to simmer until the syrup reaches a hard crack stage or until a candy thermometer inserted into the syrup reads 300°F.

Remove the pan from the heat and gently add the peanuts and baking soda. Transfer the mixture to your prepared baking sheet and spread to ¼-inch thickness. Sprinkle the crushed peanut pieces over the top.

The brittle will harden as it cools. Allow to cool completely before breaking into desired shapes, about 1 hour. Store in an airtight container at room temperature for up to a week.

These fritters are a simple way to use over-ripened bananas or plantains. Finely milled corn or tapioca flour binds the crushed pieces of banana together. The fritters can be sweetened with honey or powdered sugar or made savory by adding minced onion and chile to the batter. Best served hot out of the fryer, these fritters are also an easy addition to your small chops platter.

Mosa (Ripe Banana or Plantain Fritters)

YIELD: 30 FRITTERS

1 cup stone-ground yellow cornmeal

⅓ cup all-purpose flour

1 teaspoon baking powder

¼ teaspoon baking soda

1 teaspoon kosher salt

1 pound very ripe plantains (black skin)

2 scallions, root ends trimmed, green and white part thinly sliced

1 teaspoon grated garlic

1 tablespoon grated ginger

1 red Scotch bonnet pepper, minced with seeds, or 1 teaspoon red pepper flakes

6 tablespoons sour cream

In a medium bowl, whisk together the cornmeal, flour, baking powder, baking soda and salt.

Cut off the tips of each plantain. Use a sharp knife to create a slit in the skin along the length of each plantain, carefully making sure not to cut into the flesh. Remove peels and discard. Slice plantains into 1-inch-thick pieces.

Using a mortar and pestle or a food processor, pound or pulse the plantain pieces into a coarse puree. Avoid making the puree too smooth especially if using a food processor.

Stir the scallions, grated garlic, ginger, and Scotch bonnet or pepper flakes into the puree. Add the plantain mixture into the cornmeal mix and stir until the batter is just combined and resembles a shaggy dough. Fold in the sour cream.

Line a sheet pan with a layer of paper towels or insert with a baking rack for draining. Heat 1½ inches of oil in a medium but deep skillet over medium-high to 350°F.

Working in batches without overcrowding the pan, drop teaspoon sized portions of the batter into the hot oil and fry, turning frequently until golden brown, 5 minutes total. Maintain the temperature of the oil during the fry process by raising or lowering the heat as needed.

Transfer the mosa to the prepared sheet pan using a slotted spoon or pair of tongs. Repeat the frying process with the remaining batter until it is all used up.

Serve warm.

Kokoro is a savory fried snack made from a soft cornmeal dough that is shaped by hand into long rods and fried. I've incorporated chile powder in the dough here, but feel free to omit if you prefer a milder snack.

Kokoro

YIELD: 1 DOZEN

2 cups finely ground cornmeal

1 tablespoon sugar

½ teaspoon ground cayenne pepper

½ teaspoon baking powder

½ teaspoon salt

1 tablespoon Manshanu (page 96), melted

Oil, for frying

Into a medium bowl, combine the cornmeal, sugar, cayenne, baking powder, and salt and whisk to incorporate. Add the melted manshanu and stir. Pour in ¾ cups water and use your fingers to incorporate the flour into a smooth dough. Divide the dough into 12 equal portions. Allow the dough to rest for about 10 minutes.

Roll each portion of dough between your hands into a long strip, 8 to 10 inches. As you roll, try to achieve a ½-inch thickness, similar in shape to a painter's brush or a thin breadstick. You should have 12 dough rods when you're finished.

Heat the oil in a fryer, large stockpot, or Dutch oven to 350°F. Fry the dough rods in batches until golden brown, about 5 to 6 minutes. Using tongs, move the rods to a plate lined with paper towels or a cooling rack inserted in a baking sheet to drain. Allow to cool before serving.

I encountered danqua for the first time while sitting in Lagos traffic. There's a roundabout on Agidingbi Road heading back to my parents' house that is notoriously congested during rush hour. I noticed these golden rolls of dough wrapped in plastic bags sold streetside by vendors, and was intrigued by the color and textured round shapes on display. Call me a captive audience, an impulse purchaser, or a curiosity seeker: My first bite converted me into a believer.

Danqua, also known as dankwa or tanfiri, is a combination of ground dry-roasted peanuts, roasted cornmeal, a sweetener, and a mix of warming spices such as ginger powder and cayenne. When made fresh, it is a pleasantly spicy nut butter firm enough to roll or scoop into individual portions. A few bites of this buttery, earthy confection helped sustain me when I was pregnant, and afterwards whenever I felt an insatiable hunger while nursing.

Danqua will keep stored at room temperature in an airtight container for up to a week, refrigerated for up to 2 weeks, or frozen for a month.

Danqua /Dankwa

YIELD: ABOUT 40 PIECES

3 cups fine or medium ground yellow cornmeal

4 cups whole raw peanuts (or 600g unsalted peanut butter)

½ cup granulated sugar

1½ tablespoons ground ginger

½ teaspoon ground cayenne pepper

Pinch ground nutmeg

Pinch ground cloves

2 tablespoons roasted peanut oil

For the Roasted Cornmeal
In a large skillet set over medium heat, add in the cornmeal. Toast, stirring frequently until the cornmeal is fragrant and nutty, and turns a light brown, about 15 minutes. Remove from the skillet and transfer to a bowl to cool completely. Transfer to an airtight container and store at room temp for up to a month.

For the Danqua/Dankwa
In the bowl of a food processor, blend the peanuts to a paste. Move the peanut paste to a bowl and add 1 cup roasted cornmeal, the sugar, ginger, cayenne pepper, nutmeg, cloves, and peanut oil. Mix until incorporated. It should come together to form a dough.

Scoop tablespoon-size portions of dough and roll into balls (you can also use an ice cream scoop). Store in an airtight container in the refrigerator or freezer for up to a month.

I've never encountered gurudi as a homemade snack, but have mostly seen it in bright orange and blue plastic packs that read "Funtime Coconut Chips," and that's exactly what it is: a fun time.

After moving to the United States where there is no gurudi (homemade or otherwise), I began to think it was some mystical product that only the confectioners back home could concoct. My mum, however, set me straight: the ingredients were things I had on hand, and the steps to make it relatively easy. So here's my recipe for gurudi, a taste of home in the simplest of combinations: grated coconut, a sweetener, a little warm spice, and cassava starch or tapioca flour.

You may find that when the gurudi is warm and just out of the oven, the sheet is pliable. This is the time to cut it into neat little squares, if you want clean edges. I prefer to wait until the sheet is completely cooled and crack it into uneven pieces.

Gurudi

SERVES 8 TO 10

Coconut oil, for brushing

1 cup unsweetened finely shredded coconut flakes

¾ cup cornstarch

¼ cup sugar

½ teaspoon salt

¼ teaspoon nutmeg or other spice

Preheat the oven to 325°F. Brush a baking sheet or 9 x 13-inch cake pan with a light coat of coconut oil.

In a medium bowl, combine the coconut flakes, cornstarch, sugar, salt, and nutmeg with 1 cup of water. Spread the batter in your prepared baking sheet or pan thin enough to touch all the edges of the pan. Bake until the edges and surface are a nice golden brown and the cookie is set, about 12 minutes. Remove the pan from the oven and allow it to cool completely. Once cooled, break into pieces to serve.

This cookie can be stored at room temperature in an airtight container for up to 1 week.

NOTE This confection is indebted to Afro-Brazilian influence on Lagos Island cuisine. Coconut with a hint of nutmeg carries a coastal essence that evokes other dishes that connect Lagosians to Afro-Brazilians, like Frejon (page 199) and Kanjika (page 256).

This is another Lagos Island dessert that reminds me of my grandmother, who served this every Easter. A rich and cooling pudding, kanjika is made of fermented cornstarch (page 42) cooked in fresh coconut milk, sweetened with sugar, and chilled until firm enough to slice. Cold cubes of kanjika right out of the refrigerator are irresistible on a hot humid day. Kanjika can be garnished with cinnamon, nutmeg, or both. Topped with cubes of cold fruit and a simple mint syrup, this pudding is the perfect sweet ending to a meal.

Kanjika
WITH FRUIT

SERVES 4 TO 6

3 cups full-fat coconut milk

1 cup fresh Ògi (page 42) or 1½ cups dry ògi powder

¼ cup sugar

½ teaspoon fine salt

½ teaspoon grated nutmeg or ground cinnamon

2 cups chopped cold fresh fruit such as papaya, mango, citrus segments, berries

Mint Simple Syrup (see Note, page 266)

In a small bowl, combine the coconut milk with the ògi paste (or powder), sugar, and salt. Whisk to dissolve completely. Transfer to a small saucepan over low heat, stirring constantly until the mixture thickens and bubbles slowly begin to rise to the surface, about 8 minutes. Reduce the heat to low, and allow the pudding to steam until all the starch is completely cooked through and the mixture turns opaque, about 4 minutes.

Remove the pudding from the heat, pour into your dish or pan, and sprinkle on the nutmeg or cinnamon. Allow the kanjika to set completely in the refrigerator to chill, 4 to 8 hours. Serve topped with pieces of cold fruit and a drizzle of mint simple syrup.

When Yemi and I began collaborating on dinners, the menus were planned based on what I knew she was growing. She showed up one summer with bundles of fresh, fragrant lemongrass—so reminiscent of my parents' garden—and I knew I needed a dish that could highlight the aroma of this versatile plant.

My approach to this dessert is to allow each element to shine. I love the uniqueness of tapioca prepared this way. Opaque caviar-like beads of cooked cassava starch are immersed in a broth. I'm endlessly pleased by its slippery, gummy texture. Combined with the roasted pineapples, the sweet-salty lemongrass coconut milk, rich dark honey for depth, and a garnish of fresh grass for a little pop of green, this is a last course to cool and calm the palate after a fiery meal, or to enjoy as a midday snack.

Tapioca WITH FRUIT AND LEMONGRASS COCONUT MILK

SERVES 4

TAPIOCA

1 tablespoon sugar

Fine salt to taste

1 cup small pearl tapioca

LEMONGRASS COCONUT MILK

2½ cups unsweetened coconut milk

2-ounce bunch of fresh lemongrass or 2 lemongrass stalks

2-inch piece of ginger, scrubbed and thinly sliced

¼ cup scent leaf, plus more for garnish

4 loose cups diced fresh ripe mango (about 2 mangoes, peeled and cut into 1-inch squares)

1 tablespoon honey, plus more for drizzling

Zest and juice of 2 limes

Caramelized pineapple, for serving

CARAMELIZED PINEAPPLE
(About 4 servings)

1½ cups/ 300 grams granulated sugar

1 small fresh pineapple, peeled, cored and cut into cubes

½ teaspoon fine salt

For the Lemongrass Coconut Milk

Rinse out the small pot and pour in the coconut milk. Add the lemongrass and the ginger. Bring to a simmer over medium heat. Add the scent leaves, including the stems, and remove from the heat. Allow the infused milk to steep while you prepare the fruit.

In a blender, puree the diced mango, honey, lime zest, 2 tablespoons lime juice, and a pinch of salt. Blend until smooth, taste, and adjust the seasoning with more lime juice and salt if necessary.

Strain the coconut milk using a fine-mesh sieve, pressing down on the aromatics in the sieve before discarding.

To serve, divide the fruit puree among shallow bowls. Top with spoonfuls of the tapioca. Pour in the infused coconut milk. Drizzle more honey on top and garnish with scent leaves. Serve immediately alongside caramelized pineapple.

For the Caramelized Pineapple

Heat a large skillet over medium heat. Add the sugar and cook, stirring frequently, until it becomes a light golden syrup, 5 to 6 minutes. Continue to cook to a deeper golden brown, about 1 minute more. Carefully add the fruit and reduce the heat to medium-low. The hot syrup may bubble and become foamy.

Once the bubbling slows (after about a minute), add the salt and stir the mixture to melt any hard chunks of caramel that have formed, about 2 minutes. Remove from heat and allow the pineapple pieces to steep in the caramel syrup until they are infused, at least 30 minutes (or up to overnight in the refrigerator). The pineapple will turn a deeper yellow as it steeps. Caramelized pineapple can be made up to 1 week ahead, stored in the syrup in an airtight container for up to 1 week.

For the Tapioca

In a small pot, bring 2 cups of water to a boil and add the sugar and a pinch of salt. Stir in the tapioca pearls and simmer gently over low heat until the tapioca is cooked through, opaque, and softened, about 10 minutes. Transfer to a bowl and refrigerate until ready to serve.

Millet is popular in many forms, and this drink of fura combined with nono—a kefir or yogurt—is a dish from northern Nigeria, where millet is cooked and dried in a way that doesn't require refrigeration. In Lagos and across Nigeria, fura de nono is served in homes and sold by vendors on the street. Vendors will often crush the cooked and dried millet paste into the kefir to order, and the intermingling textures and flavors are delightfully invigorating.

This recipe skips the step of air-drying the cooked millet paste, but if you make it ahead, store the paste in the refrigerator until you're ready to go. I make homemade yogurt (page 121), which is similar to traditional nono. If you want to skip this step, combine the fura with three cups whole milk blended with one cup of thick, tangy yogurt.

Fura de Nono

**YIELD: 4 SERVINGS,
AND 12 COOKED MILLET BALLS**

MILLET PASTE

2 cups Fura
(fermented millet
paste, page 45)

1 tablespoon
Toasted Spice
Blend for Sweets
(page 101)

DRINK

4 cups kefir,
yogurt, or milk

¼ cup honey

½ teaspoon salt

Pour the fermented millet paste in a medium pot, add the spice blend, and place over medium-low heat. Cook the starch, stirring frequently with a wooden spoon to prevent the bottom from scorching, until the paste thickens, 6 minutes. Once cooked, add ⅓ cup of water, cover the pot and cook for 4 minutes until the dough changes from cloudy to translucent.

Divide the dough into 12 portions by dropping tablespoons

of the dough onto a baking sheet or large plate. Shape each portion into rounds and allow to cool completely. At this point, the cooked millet balls can be stored refrigerated in an airtight container for up to 1 week.

To make the drink, combine 4 millet balls with the kefir, honey, and salt in a blender or food processor. Puree until smooth. Pour into bowls or mugs and serve immediately.

DRINKS

Drinks can refresh, heighten, or neutralize our sense of taste. At their best, they give the palate another opportunity to engage with fresh ingredients. Along with the rest of the world's cities, Lagos has recently been swept up in a cocktail craze. To Lagos's benefit, the ingredients we can obtain locally add extraordinary complexity to popular drinks.

This chapter is called Drinks, but it's not held together by the best or most popular beverages you'll find on menus across Lagos. These recipes highlight the evolution of beverage culture throughout Nigeria and embrace traditional ingredients in new ways. These drinks are based on ingredients I love and are perfect for entertaining guests at my dinners or in my home. This is not the definitive guide to what Lagosians drink, but a sample of what I enjoy and have enjoyed while living in Nigeria.

Just as we do with the rest of our cuisine, Lagosians (and Nigerians in general) approach beverages without a strict adherence to category. There isn't a definitive guide to Nigerian cocktails, as far as I'm aware, and the category of "soft drinks"— or beverages without alcohol—is as capacious as an encyclopedia. Sodas based in malted grains are as common as those based in citrus ingredients. Teas are made with herbs, dried fruits, and sometimes leaves, barks, stems, and the roots of trees and shrubs. I have a cabinet full of locally sourced barks and branches that, when brewed, yield teas with wonderfully rich flavors and medicinal properties. Fruits such as pineapple, mango, and citrus are common ingredients in juices, as is sugarcane. Nuts, seeds, and kernels from a variety of plants are pressed and filtered to make milks and bases for other drinks.

Fermented beverages are common across Nigeria, and their base ingredients vary by culture and region: dairy, corn, grains, and palm sap are all produced and consumed in varying stages of fermentation. Palm sap is often fermented into palm wine, a beverage with a long history and much ceremonial importance across the south of Nigeria. But its formula can vary by region and producer, with alcohol percentages that range from barely perceptible to the strength of a gin or whiskey. A drink we call òǵóǵóró, a strong palm-sap-based spirit found across West Africa, is another example of one of our more potent brews.

The recipes that follow are guided by whatever fruits, herbs, extracts, and fermentations one can find easily in Lagos. There is a lot of Yewande in this chapter and my penchant for something a little sweet, a little herbal, and a little boozy is prominently displayed.

Simple Syrups for Drinks and Cocktails

Think of these syrups as building blocks for the cocktails to follow. They can be made and stored in the refrigerator up to a week in advance.

Ginger and Buckwheat Honey Syrup

YIELD: 1 PINT

1 cup buckwheat honey or other dark honey

3-inch piece of ginger, grated

Zest of 1 lemon

Combine the honey, 1 cup water, ginger, and lemon zest into a small saucepan and bring to a boil, stirring to ensure the honey fully dissolves. Lower heat to a simmer for 10 additional minutes, stirring occasionally. Set aside and allow to cool completely. Strain through a fine-mesh strainer. Store in an airtight container in the refrigerator for up to 3 weeks.

Bitter Lemon Syrup

YIELD: 1 PINT

1½ cups granulated sugar

¼ cup dried lemon verbena

5 ounces lemon juice

Zest of 2 lemons

Combine 1 cup water, sugar, and lemon verbena in a small saucepan. Bring to a boil and turn off the heat. Add the lemon juice and zest. Let steep for 15 to 20 minutes and strain through a fine-mesh strainer. Store in an airtight container in the refrigerator for up to 2 weeks.

Lemongrass and Spice Simple Syrup

1 cup granulated sugar

2 stalks of lemongrass, smashed

2 tablespoons Toasted Spice Blend for Sweets (see page 101)

(see page 101)

YIELD: 1½ CUPS

Combine the sugar, 1 cup water, lemongrass, and toasted spice blend into a small saucepan and bring to a boil. Lower heat and simmer for 15 minutes. Set aside and allow to cool completely. Strain through a fine-mesh strainer. Store in an airtight container in the refrigerator for up to 3 weeks.

Hibiscus Simple Syrup

¼ cup dried hibiscus

1 cup granulated sugar

YIELD: 1½ CUPS

Add the hibiscus and 1 cup water to a small saucepan and bring to a boil. Remove from the heat, add the sugar, and return to a boil, stirring to ensure the sugar is incorporated. Remove from the heat and let cool completely. Strain through a fine-mesh strainer. Store in an airtight container in the refrigerator for up to 3 weeks.

NOTE: MINT SIMPLE SYRUP Substitute 1 cup of fresh mint leaves for the hibiscus.

Cane-Infused Simple Syrup

One 6- to 8-inch stalk of sugarcane, washed and scrubbed

½ cup granulated sugar

NOTE This is not a recipe for sugarcane syrup, which is a syrup of reduced sugarcane juice. That is a process beyond what most of us can achieve in a home kitchen. Think of this as a simple syrup with an infusion of fresh cane juice. This recipe also allows you to reuse your sugarcane as garnish, as they'll still be packed with plenty of sweet juice.

YIELD: 3 CUPS

Use a sharp knife to quarter the sugarcane lengthwise and cut each quarter into 2- to 3-inch pieces. In a medium saucepan, add the cut cane to 3 cups water and bring to a boil. Lower to a simmer and keep simmering for 30 minutes. Remove from the heat and strain the mixture into a large Pyrex (or similar heat-resistant) liquid measure. If you have less than 2 cups of liquid, add water until you reach 2 cups.

Return the liquid to the saucepan and add in the granulated sugar. You can also add the sugarcane back at this stage. Halving each piece of sugar cane before doing so will help them release more juice, but run them under cold water before attempting to slice them. Bring the mixture to a boil and then remove from the heat. Allow to cool completely. Store in an airtight container in the refrigerator for up to 3 weeks. Use the sugarcane pieces as drink garnishes.

This simple granita can be used as an intermezzo or as part of a dessert course. It carries citrus and fruit notes from the baobab and orange, as well as a little bite from the selim pepper.

Baobab Coconut Amuse

SERVES 10

12 ounces unsweetened coconut milk

2 tablespoons honey

1 tablespoon baobab powder

1 teaspoon selim pepper

Zest from 1 orange

Combine the coconut milk, honey, baobab powder, selim pepper, and orange zest into a blender and pulse until well incorporated. Pour the mixture into a baking pan and let set in the freezer for 30 minutes. Every 10 minutes, move a fork through the mixture to give the amuse a granita-like texture.

This is my afternoon beverage in Lagos. I am usually so focused on refreshment that I forget to prepare myself for the sharpness of the lemon and quinine; it quite literally snaps me out of my midday fog. Bitter lemon soda from a variety of brands is everywhere in Lagos, but this is the recipe I rely on at home in Brooklyn, where bitter lemon is much harder to find.

Bitter Lemon Soda

SERVES 1

1½ ounces Bitter Lemon Syrup (see page 265)

6 ounces tonic water, chilled

Lime wedge as garnish

Combine the bitter lemon syrup with chilled tonic water in a tall glass and stir gently. Add ice and a lime wedge to garnish.

A chapman is not an all-seasons drink in the United States, but Lagos weather is always suitable for one. In the late afternoon or early evening, there is nothing quite like this heroically sweet blend of citrus and fizz. In this version, I've swapped out standard ingredients like orange soda, lemon-lime soda, and grenadine for orange juice, bitter lemon syrup, and hibiscus simple syrup.

House Chapman

SERVES 1

2 ounces
orange juice

2 ounces Bitter
Lemon Syrup
(page 265)

1½ ounces Hibiscus
Simple Syrup
(page 266)

6 ounces club
soda

1 orange slice
as garnish

4 cucumber slices
as garnish

Combine the orange juice, bitter lemon syrup, hibiscus syrup, and club soda into a glass. Add ice and garnish with orange and cucumber slices. Serve immediately.

Tamarind Cooler

SERVES 1

1 ounce Tamarind
Paste (page 98)

2 ounces Ginger
and Buckwheat
Honey Syrup
(page 265)

½ teaspoon salt

6 ounces soda
water

Combine the tamarind paste, honey syrup, and salt into a tall glass. Add the soda water slowly, stirring gently to incorporate. Add ice and serve immediately.

Pineapple Drink

SERVES 1

6 ounces fresh
pineapple juice

2 ounces
Lemongrass and
Spice Simple
Syrup (page 266)

Club soda

Mint sprigs
as garnish

Pour the pineapple juice and simple syrup into a wineglass. Add ice, top with the club soda, and stir. Garnish with sprigs of mint. Serve immediately.

COCKTAILS

Each of my dinner parties begins with an hour devoted to sampling small chops right out of the kitchen and a choice of three distinct cocktails. I try to incorporate flavor elements from my dishes into the drinks I serve, and this time is crucial for acclimating my guests to the sensory experiences to follow. These are in no way meant to be traditional Lagosian cocktails, although they are based in beverages most Nigerians encounter in bukas and markets. Lagos's cocktail culture is in full swing, and whether you're lounging on an outdoor hotel patio on Victoria Island or catching a performance at a mainland venue, these are the perfect drinks to wrap up a long day in traffic, in cues, or at the office. Each of these cocktails should be accompanied by generous amounts of Nigerian highlife classics, afropop, or hip-hop.

V.I. Special (Rye with Malta and Orange)

2 ounces rye or other whiskey

1 ounces Ginger and Buckwheat Honey Syrup (page 265)

Dash of bitters

2 ounces Malta

Orange peel as garnish

SERVES 1

Combine the rye, honey syrup, and bitters into a cocktail strainer and pour into a rocks glass over ice, top with Malta, and garnish with an orange peel.

Hibiscus Sisi

1 ounce fresh lime juice

Mint leaves

Cucumber slices

1½ ounces Hibiscus Simple Syrup (page 266)

2 ounces òɡóɡóró (or any neutral spirit such as gin or vodka)

Mint sprig, cucumber slice, and orange slice

2 ounces club soda or sparkling wine, for serving

SERVES 1

To a cocktail shaker, add the lime juice, mint leaves, and cucumber slices and use a cocktail muddler to gently break down the cucumber and mint. Add the hibiscus simple syrup, òɡóɡóró, and ice. Shake well and strain over ice into a wineglass. Garnish with a mint sprig, cucumber slice, and orange slice. Top with chilled club soda or sparkling wine to serve.

Palm Wine Spritz

3 ounces palm wine

½ ounce triple sec

1 ounce Cane-Infused Simple Syrup (page 266)

2 ounces club soda

Sliver of sugarcane or orange slice as garnish

SERVES 1

Add the palm wine, triple sec, and simple syrup to a cocktail shaker. Add ice and stir until chilled. Add to a champagne flute and top with club soda. Garnish with a sliver of sugarcane or an orange slice.

Palm wine is derived from the sap of certain palm tree species. It ferments in the open air and can be consumed within a few days when tapped fresh. However, most palm wine in the diaspora is a palm-derived product that is distilled, sweetened, and bottled for mass production. Taking nothing away from those who love their palm wine tapped straight from the tree (as it has been traditionally produced for centuries), this recipe incorporates the bottled palm wine found in supermarkets, African grocers, and the food and beverage businesses Nigerians have established across the diaspora. Served as a spritz with my sugar cane syrup, it is a refreshing beverage for any time of year.

There are many ways to incorporate this tonic into your routine: as an ingredient in a smoothie, an after-meal digestif, or a simple refreshment. I have become obsessed with tonics now that I have more access to greens and other produce from my friend Yemi's farm. It seems that once we have our native herbs and greens within reach, we start to explore all the ways to center our health and nutrition in ancestral traditions. Whereas the greens Yemi grows are great for blood and cardiovascular health, this tonic shares many common ingredients of other immunity-boosting tonics. It is rich with vitamin C, digestive aids, and anti-inflammatory properties.

Citrus Health Tonic

3 oranges, sliced

3 limes, sliced

1 lemon, sliced

3-inch piece of ginger, grated

2 stalks of lemongrass

1 teaspoon turmeric

Honey, to taste (optional)

SERVES 4 TO 6

Combine the oranges, limes, lemon, ginger, lemongrass, and turmeric into a large saucepan with 4 cups water and bring to a boil. Lower the heat and simmer for 5 minutes. Turn off the heat and let steep for 15 to 20 minutes. Strain through a large-mesh strainer or chinois.

To serve, pour 4 to 6 ounces into a small glass and stir in honey, if desired.

Àṣẹ́

Olódùmarè, Orí mi, Egbe mi, Eegún, Orisa, mojùbà. Ire o!

I would like to take a moment to share my deepest appreciation for the people who have helped make *My Everyday Lagos* a reality.

A'a e e wowo di l'otu e m a le gbe un—No matter how heavy the body may be, the owner will still be able to carry it.

To myself: The process of writing *My Everyday Lagos* granted me all the joys and challenges of true self-discovery. I am grateful I believed in myself. To all the versions of myself I had to gather to complete this project, we are safe now. To my body, thank you for allowing us to see this through. To my spirit, may we always be. Àṣẹ́

Ijo je o we yon i—Eating together makes the exercise enjoyable.

To my life partner, Mark Losinger: Thank you for the love, the safety, and most of all for accompanying me on this journey. To our fierce, sweet Aṣa and deliberate, darling Midé: Everything you need exists within you. Thank you both for choosing us. To my parents, Oluwole and Omotunde Komolafe, and my brothers, Olumide Komolafe and Oluseeni Komolafe. To my extended family, Bill Losinger, Judy Kaplowitz, Sue and Charles Keller: You have given me so much love, and I have drawn from it along the way. Our shared meals have informed and shaped so much of me and so much of this book. I deeply appreciate you all.

Ẹyẹ ò lè fi apá kan fò— Birds cannot fly with only one wing.

To my diaspora fam: Olamide Fadiora, Yemi Amu, Steph Yawa De Wolfe, George McCalman, Princess Yewande

Olowu, Micheal Elegbede, Hawa Hassan, Akintunde Wey, Busayo Olupona: Random calls that last longer than we planned, catching up over good food and drinks, laughter at the many wonders life has thrown at us. This is the everyday spirit that I have tried to capture in this book. Thank you all for being a part of my life and helping me get to this beautiful place.

A ki í fi ò nà ikùn han ò fun—One does not show the throat the way to the stomach.

I must praise the amazing team of experts that have guided my hand and the fruits of my labor. Agent Kari Stuart and the family at CAA. Art director George McCalman and his wonderful assistant, Aliena Cameron. Team Photo: Kelly Marshall, Gerri Williams, Jillian Knox, Melina Kemph, Brittany Darty, Megan Branagh, Caroline Lange. Location photography: Lola Akinmade. Illustrations: Diana Ejaita. Editorial team: Yemi Amu, Steph Yawa De Wolfe, Micheal Elegbede, Ozoz Sokoh, Alexis Cheung, Hannane Ferdjani.

And of course, the Ten Speed Press team members: my editor, Dervla Kelly; editorial assistant Gabby Urena; design manager Betsy Stromberg; production manager Jane Chinn; production editor Mark McCauslin; production designers Mari Gill and Faith Hague; prepress color manager Nick Patton; copyeditor Nancy Bailey; proofreaders Lisa Lawley, Jacob Sammon, Abby Oladipo, and Penelope Haynes; indexer Elizabeth Parson; publicist Kristin Casemore; and marketer Brianne Sperber.

Àṣẹ

Index

Published in the United States by Ten Speed Press, an imprint of the
Crown Publishing Group, a division of Penguin Random House LLC, New York.
TenSpeed.com

Ten Speed Press and the Ten Speed Press colophon are registered trademarks
of Penguin Random House LLC.

Typefaces: Adobe's Caslon Pro, Hoefler & Frere-Jones's Gotham,
and George McCalman's Yewande

Library of Congress Cataloging-in-Publication Data is on file with the publisher.

Hardcover ISBN: 978-1-9848-5893-1
Ebook ISBN: 978-1-9848-5894-8

Printed in China

Editor: Dervla Kelly | Production editor: Mark McCauslin
Art director and designer: George McCalman | Associate designer: Aliena Cameron
Design manager: Betsy Stromberg
Production designers: Mari Gill and Faith Hague
Production manager: Jane Chinn | Prepress color manager: Nick Patton
Copyeditor: Nancy Bailey | Indexer: Elizabeth T. Parson
Proofreaders: Lisa Lawley, Jacob Sammon, Abby Oladipo, Penelope Haynes
Publicist: Kristin Casemore | Marketer: Brianne Sperber

10 9 8 7 6 5 4 3 2 1

First Edition